Trudeau on Trudeau

THE DEEP THOUGHTS OF CANADA'S 23rd PRIME MINISTER

Ian Ferguson

PUBLISHED BY SIMON & SCHUSTER

New York London Toronto Sydney New Delhi

SIMON &
SCHUSTER
CANADA

Simon & Schuster Canada
A Division of Simon & Schuster, Inc.
166 King Street East, Suite 300
Toronto, Ontario M5A 1J3

This Simon & Schuster Canada edition September 2019

SIMON & SCHUSTER CANADA and colophon are trademarks
of Simon & Schuster, Inc.

For information about special discounts for bulk purchases,
please contact Simon & Schuster Special Sales at 1-800-268-3216
or CustomerService@simonandschuster.ca.

Interior design by Silverglass

Manufactured in the United States of America

10 9 8 7 6 5 4 3 2 1

Library and Archives Canada Cataloguing in Publication
Title: Trudeau on Trudeau: the deep thoughts of Canada's 23rd prime minister /
    by Ian Ferguson.
  Names: Ferguson, Ian, 1959– author.
  Identifiers: Canadiana (print) 20190069813 | Canadiana (ebook) 20190069899 |
ISBN 9781982123680 (softcover) | ISBN 9781982123697 (ebook)
  Subjects: LCSH: Trudeau, Justin—Humor. | LCSH: Trudeau, Justin—Quotations. |
LCSH: Trudeau, Justin—
  Language. | LCSH: Malapropisms.
  Classification: LCC FC655 .F47 2019 | DDC 971.07/4—dc23

ISBN 978-1-9821-2368-0
ISBN 978-1-9821-2369-7 (ebook)

"*Life is a state of mind.*"
Jerzy Kosiński, *Being There*

Contents

Trudeau on Trudeau

Introduction

How Did We Get Here?

The Bollywood dance moves. The $50 million tweet to impress an American TV host. Justin's professed admiration for China's "basic dictatorship." His breezy assurances that "the budget will balance itself." (He inherited a surplus, remember.) Found guilty of breaching Canada's ethics laws not once, not twice, but *four times*. Mocked at home and abroad for coining the word *peoplekind*, to say nothing of *responsibilizing*. The goofy socks. The constant bragging about how humble he is. The endless, endless selfies.

How did this happen? How did it all go so horribly wrong? To answer this question, I turned to a higher authority:

SIRI, WHAT HAPPENS IF YOU PUT A FORMER SNOWBOARD INSTRUCTOR AND PART-TIME DRAMA TEACHER IN CHARGE OF A G7 ECONOMY?

Siri whirred and clicked and spat out the following actual headlines, all of which ran within a few weeks of each other in 2018 alone.

CANADA'S STOCK MARKET IS THE WORST IN THE WORLD RIGHT NOW
MoneySense

•

THE CANADIAN DOLLAR IS THE WORST PERFORMING MAJOR CURRENCY IN THE WORLD THIS YEAR
CBC News

•

JUSTIN TRUDEAU'S BUDGET STILL HASN'T BALANCED ITSELF
London Free Press

•

SCIENCE-LOVING GOVERNMENT CUTS FUNDING FOR SCIENCE
Globe and Mail

•

TRUDEAU'S PERPETUAL DEFICITS WILL CAUSE LASTING HARM
Winnipeg Sun

•

I'll admit it. I was caught up in the giddy excitement of Justin too.

He was *sooo* dreamy. Nice hair. Famous dad. True, he had absolutely no background in economics or law (or ethics, apparently), but who cares! He was a new type of politician. One created for and elected by social media. Prime Minister Selfie to the rescue! Yay! My greatest claim to fame? I'm one of only three people in Canada who has never had a selfie taken with Justin Trudeau.

But then he got elected, and I realized that the economy does in fact affect me, that deficits aren't magical numbers sprinkled with pixie dust and feigned sincerity, that it's not just style that matters, but substance too. How did it go so wrong? Let us consult the experts, and there is no bigger expert on Justin Trudeau than Justin Himself.

Here, then, is Canada's prime minister in his own words. All of the quotes that follow are real; all are fully sourced at the back of this book. You can easily find them online as well. In most cases, you can watch him sharing these bon mots on CPAC, CBC, CTV, Global, and so on. Just in case you think any of this is exaggerated, it's not. In fact, I urge you to go online and view these firsthand. But be prepared, once you fall down the rabbit hole of Justin Speak, you may never re-emerge, certainly not with your innocence intact.

Canada, we elected Zoolander as prime minister. This one is on us. We have no one else to blame but ourselves.

Frat Boy

FRAT BOYS LOVE FUN. **BEER-LOVING FUN.**

Remember that time Justin Trudeau was accused of groping a reporter? Of course you don't. It was quickly swept under the rug. And anyway, it happened at a drunken beer fest in BC years ago, so who cares? Part of the frat boy code, right? Frat boys love the ladies. And beer. They also love beer.

What is Justin's one tangible achievement, the one thing no one can take away from him? He legalized weed. Party on, bro!

"The intensity, the excitement of being in the middle of a political campaign—it's heavy, it's fun stuff. There's pizza, sex, and all sorts of fun things."

"I don't read the newspapers, I don't watch the news. I figure, if something important happens, someone will tell me."

"People in the street will either call me 'Prime Minister' or 'Justin.' We'll see how that goes. But when I'm working, when I'm with my staff in public, I'm 'Prime Minister.' I say that if we're drinking beer out of a bottle, and you can see my tattoos, you should be comfortable calling me 'Justin.'"

"It's very, very cool to have the president call up, and I say, 'Hello, Mr. President.'"

OMG! Justin talks about that time Barack Obama called him on the phone.

Unfortunately, although it is readily available online, we aren't allowed to show you the now famous photo of Justin Trudeau partying onstage at the Kokanee Beer Fest, where allegations of groping and inappropriate behaviour first surfaced. Instead, please enjoy the above photo as an approximate replacement. Cheers!

"I'm not going to go around reciting pi to the 19th decibel."

Take that people who say Justin is not so smarter as other peoples!!

"I'm going to defer to scientists."

Justin Trudeau on tricky scientific notions.

He had been asked whether the North Pole was part of Canada. This is a crucial point, because we share access to the pole with several countries, including Russia. (As anyone with a globe can tell you.) How this would be settled by "scientists" remains unclear.

"They will come at me on my judgement because I offered, literally, my shirt to a charity, the Canadian Liver Foundation. Or, you know, for various cancers that I parade around as my evil twin with my own moustache."

Justin employs the Matthew McConaughey defence: "Sure, I take my shirt off, but it's for a good cause."

*J*ustin was famously invited to a sultry "Ladies Only" event.

Now, we are not permitted to show you the actual invitation, but we can give you a *feel* of it . . .

Picture soft pink and pastel images of a dreamy Justin . . .

A flowery cursive font beckons . . . Cocktails, conversation, a whisper in the ear: *"Ladies only . . ."*

"What happens if I drop an anvil on a watermelon?"

The prime minister of Canada, ladies and gentlemen!

This is Justin showing us how cool and relatable he is to young people. It was part of a long, rambling stage-managed event where he famously said, "Babies are scientists," and then went on to discuss cool YouTube videos with children's TV host Bill Nye the Science Guy. Onstage. For real. This really happened.

*S*peaking of dropping anvils on watermelons . . . That event with Bill Nye the Science Guy, held at the University of Ottawa, was titled "Investing in Canadian Innovation." Which raises the question: Why did the government fly in an *American* TV host to speak with Justin Trudeau? Don't we have science personalities of our own? David Suzuki, for example. Why didn't they call on Canada's own David Suzuki instead?

"Twerp."

David Suzuki's assessment of Justin Trudeau.

Oh right. There's that.

You see, when Justin phoned Suzuki during the 2015 campaign looking for a media-friendly endorsement, Suzuki said no. "You're for the development of the tar sands, you're for the Keystone pipeline, but you're against the Northern Gateway, you're all over the damn map!" Things got heated, Justin snapped at him, and the call ended with Suzuki calling Justin a twerp and (presumably) hanging up.

But have you seen those exploding watermelons on YouTube? They are *sooo* cool!

"At one point people are going to have to realize that maybe I know what I'm doing."

Justin Trudeau: secretly competent!

Justin: Beyond Space & Time

SPACE AND TIME OR TIME AND SPACE?

During the 2015 election campaign, an online quiz asked people to guess who had said it: Derek Zoolander or Justin Trudeau? It was harder than you'd think.

The following quotes from Justin Trudeau (for example, "I'm not going to go around reciting pi to the 19th decibel" or saying there is nothing he wants more than to "create more people like me who recognize the importance of taking responsibility for the world") could easily have come from the mouth of Zoolander, a male supermodel in the comedy of the same title, a self-absorbed, not-particularly-bright narcissist who is absolutely convinced of his own profundity. (Sound familiar?)

"People come up to me all the time and say 'you should be a model,' or 'you look just like a model,' or 'maybe you should try to be a man who models.' And I always have to laugh because I'm so good looking." Compare that to "I could list a whole bunch of different challenges, and I choose not to be daunted by any of them." One is a ridiculous spoof, the other is now the prime minister of Canada. Here, then, are some of Justin's best Zoolander moments.

"We have to rethink elements as basic as space and time, to go all science fictiony on you."

Justin Trudeau urges university students in London, Ontario,
to blow their own minds.

When your prime minister legalizes marijuana, it opens up all sorts of doors into the universe, man.

"The way forward for Canada will be in a solution that resembles Canada, that is, shared values and shared desire for outcomes and different approaches to achieve those outcomes right across this great country."

Justin Trudeau on Canada's approach to climate change.

Values of desires of outcomes of approaches! Thanks for clearing that up!

"The world is moving toward more diversity, not less diversity. It's a form of entropy."

Justin Trudeau showing off his smarts.

ENTROPY ˈen-trə-pē | *n*: the degradation of matter and energy in the universe to an ultimate state of inert uniformity

So . . . kind of the opposite of increased diversity.

"There is no core identity, no mainstream in Canada."

Justin Trudeau on Canadian identity (or lack thereof).

Our Fearless Leader, ladies and gentlemen! But wait . . . if there is no core Canadian identity, how can we possibly have shared desires for outcomes of values?

"The nation is no longer a legitimate basis for the state."

Mr. Trudeau, please explain

"Responsibilizing."

Justin Trudeau on the key to effective leadership.

Remember how George "Dubya" Bush used to mangle the English language? Remember his constant malapropisms like *misunderestimate*? Oh, how we laughed and laughed! Good times, good times. Please note: Such laughter is not to be tolerated against Justin, however. If you mock Justin Trudeau, yer probably a nazi. (Note to self: Look up *peoplekind* comment, reaction to.)

Alas, once again, we were not permitted to use an iconic image of Justin, even though it is readily available online. It is an official photo taken inside his office, *Inception* style. You know the one. A photograph of a photographer taking a photograph of Justin Trudeau signing photographs . . . of himself.

"You cannot let yourself be defined by the hopes that you will fulfill the darkest wishes of your opponents."

"I'm much more focused on doing the kinds of things that demonstrate that I'm serious about what I'm doing and how I'm doing it."

On doing the things that do what you're doing! This was Justin's response to the suggestions that he is—and I quote—"a bit of a lightweight."

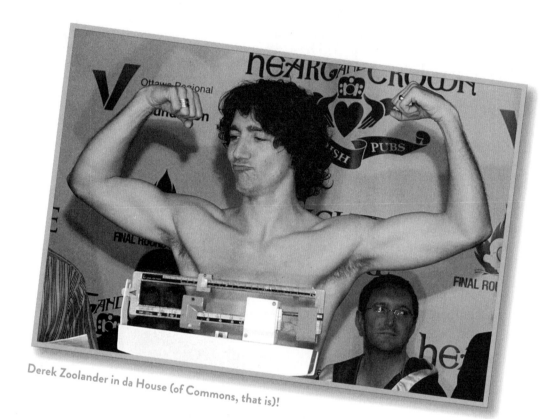

Derek Zoolander in da House (of Commons, that is)!

Justin Trudeau: International Man of Mystery!

BORN ON THIRD BASE AND THINKING
YOU HIT A TRIPLE.

If you look up *privilege* in a dictionary, there is a picture of Justin Trudeau. His grandfather was a real estate mogul, and Justin inherited a personal trust fund worth well over a million dollars, as well as shares in 90562 Canada Inc., a corporation that manages securities on behalf of the Trudeau family. He and his brother also inherited the family mansion in Montreal's Golden Square Mile.

So, when Justin rolls up his sleeves (literally; whenever he talks about "hard-working families" he first takes off his jacket and carefully rolls up his sleeves to show you just how serious he is), you know he feels your pain. Justin understands the challenges of the middle class! Why? Because he's so down to earth! How do we know he's so down to earth? Because he told us. Yay Justin!

"I won the birth lottery."

....

"We grew up in a big house, we had all sorts of advantages. All my life, I got to travel around the world, meet extraordinary people, go to great schools, have tremendous opportunities. And the one thing that was instilled in me early on was with those opportunities comes a responsibility. You need to do right by all that you've been given, and that's really how you define a person."

Because *that's* how you define a person . . .

"One of the big difficulties for me has been, all my life I've been an international traveller."

It's hard being Justin. So, so many challenges.

JUSTIN **GETS IT!**

"My maternal grandfather was born in Scotland, so I do have some idea of the challenges it takes to come to Canada and has took over the sweep of history of Canada."

Justin Trudeau on his deep, personal connection to the immigrant experience.

For the record, the grandfather Justin is referring to is James Sinclair, who came to Canada from Scotland more than one hundred years ago. Which is to say, Justin is practically one of the huddled masses himself! (As for the last line, "and has took over the sweep of history of Canada"? Your guess is as good as mine.)

BONUS JUSTIN: Justin has also suggested that his experience backpacking in various parts of the world—funded, of course, by a generous trust fund—makes him some sort of foreign affairs expert. Which is right up there with Sarah Palin's apocryphal "I can see Russia from my house!" But no mind. As anyone who has ever been trapped in a corner at a dorm-room party knows, the best authorities on world politics are always the dudes who have just, like, gotten back from backpacking through Europe, bro.

CANADA! WHERE EVEN AN UNKNOWN UNDERDOG CAN MAKE IT!

"If I'm sitting here as prime minister, it has very little to do with my last name."

Justin What's-His-Face explains to the BBC how, through mere pluck and hard work, he made it on his own, and all while facing so, so many challenges.

"Humility is very important to him."

Canadian Heritage Minister Mélanie Joly gushes about the humble modesty of her super humble boss, Justin "I won the birth lottery" Trudeau.

"There's an awful lot of people who sort of shrugged and said he has nothing but a name to go on, and found themselves slightly bewildered as I left them in the dust."

Justin, employing that renowned humility of his.

Remember, children, it had nothing to do with his famous last name or our own facile fascination with celebrity! Justin did this on his own merit, humbly. Or, as he puts it: "I left them in the dust."

ON CANADA'S **HOT LATIN BLOOD.**

"My stepfather was born in East Germany. I was raised to love German culture and German food—even the red cabbage. It's something I feel a tremendous kinship to. You are perhaps a little more . . . I'm looking for the right word—predictable? No, you're more organized, maybe, than Canadians can be. We've got enough French and Latin blood in us to be less organized."

The prime minister of Canada explains the nuances of our national character to a German news journal.

So, you can see that all that international travel hasn't gone to waste . . .

Sensei

MINDFULNESS BECOMES JUSTIN.

When he became leader of the Liberals, Justin wanted to downplay his rich-kid, frat-boy image. So he appeared in a TV commercial in front of a blackboard with complex mathematical formulas written on it, looking all frowny faced and playing up his past employment as a substitute teacher.

Watching those ads, you would be forgiven if you thought Justin had perhaps taught math in inner-city schools to underprivileged youth, rather than, say, at the tony, private West Point Grey Academy in Vancouver. And given that it was *elementary school math* he was teaching, the odds are slim that he ever taught anything close to the advanced mathematics problem he was posing in front of, but who knows? Maybe the kids at elite private schools are just smarter than the rest of us.

Justin worked as a supply, or "substitute," teacher, filling in where needed: drama, social studies, French, even elementary school math. Most of that was at a private school, true, but as Althia Raj notes in *The Contender*,

> Although Trudeau spent most of his teaching time at West Point Grey, his campaign plays down the fact that he taught mostly rich kids.
>
> During an interview with Global BC this January, in which he stressed his B.C. connections, Trudeau fibbed and said he had spent more time teaching at . . . a public school.

"There is nothing he wants to do more than try to be a teacher 'and maybe create more people like me who recognize the importance of taking responsibility for the world.'"

Justin Trudeau, as quoted in the *Globe and Mail*, back when he was still a substitute teacher, because the highest ideal one can reach is to be Justin Trudeau.

If only he could clone himself!

Note to self: Look up *narcissism disorder*, symptoms of.

"I'm a teacher; I'm a convenor; I'm a gatherer."

Justin Trudeau, self-assessment.

Justin Trudeau's favourite topic is always Justin Trudeau.

*C*urrent tuition at West Point Grey Academy, where Justin Trudeau was employed as a supply teacher:

Kindergarten–Grade 7: $20,780 a year
Grades 8–12: $22,470 a year

Which is to say, a student who attended West Point Grey Academy from grade eight to grade twelve would have to spend—lemme see, divide by six, carry the square root of twenty—$112,350.

So . . . not exactly *To Sir, With Love.*

I want someone to look at me the way
Justin Trudeau looks at everyone . . .

Meet Yer Candidate!

POP **QUIZ**

What are the two key components of overseeing a G7 economy? Taking selfies? Not quite. Photo-bombing weddings? Sorry, no. Doing one-armed push-ups? Again, no.

First and foremost, the government passes laws. That's what the government does. It's sort of the definition of *government*. Governments manage the economy and pass laws. For example, Ben Mulroney, the son of former prime minister Brian Mulroney, has a law degree from Laval and a history degree from Duke. Which is to say, he is decidedly *more* qualified to be prime minister than Justin Trudeau.

Justin *tried* to get a degree in engineering, but dropped out. *Tried* to get another degree in environmental geography, dropped out. Instead, he has an Arts degree and completed the UBC's teaching program. So, how does Justin Trudeau stack up against the competition?

*L*et us compare and contrast the leaders of Canada's main political parties. (The Green and the Bloc do not have official party status, so unfortunately aren't included here.) You can see how inadequate the leaders of the other parties are in comparison to our Justin. No wonder the media loves him so much!

Jagmeet Singh (NDP): Law degree from Osgoode Hall. Worked as a defence lawyer advocating for citizens' rights protected under the Canadian Charter of Rights and Freedoms. Provided free seminars and legal counsel to community groups and individuals in need. Helped immigrants and refugees with rights claims. Also has a degree in science (biology), which might come in handy with environmental issues and whatnot. But has Jagmeet Singh ever taught snowboarding at a ski resort in Whistler? I think not!

Andrew Scheer (Conservative): Middle-class background. Dad was a librarian. Mom was a nurse. Has a degree in History and Political Science. Is an acknowledged authority on parliamentary procedure, was the youngest Speaker of the House of Commons in Canadian history and served in that role with distinction, blah, blah, blah. But does Scheer have access to a private trust fund? No. Has Scheer ever been described as "hot"? No. Has Scheer ever posed on the cover of *Vogue* looking all pouty and dreamboaty? No, he has not.

Advantage: Justin!

HANDY CHART

Keeping this straight can be difficult, so I have included a handy chart for easy reference. By simply tallying up the check marks we can see how perfectly suited Justin is to be running the country.

	LAW DEGREE	POLITICAL SCIENCE DEGREE	FORMER SNOWBOARD INSTRUCTOR	SUBSTITUTE DRAMA TEACHER	TRUST FUND BABY
Jagmeet Singh	✓	X	X	X	X
Andrew Scheer	X	✓	X	X	X
Justin Trudeau	X	X	✓	✓	✓

One of these three men is the son of privilege *and* a former snowboarding instructor! Can you spot which one?

GREAT MOMENTS IN CANADIAN POLITICAL ORATORY #1

Who Said It: John A. Macdonald or Justin Trudeau?

....

"Let us be English, or let us be French . . . but above all let us be Canadians."

or . . .

....

"I had to learn to dismiss people who would criticize me based on nothing, but I also had to learn not to believe the people who would compliment me and think I was great based on nothing and that led me to have a very, very strong sense of myself and my strengths."

National Security Stuff

THE JOYS OF DAYTIME TV.

In 2017, Justin appeared on the popular American daytime TV program *Live with Kelly and Ryan.* (Sample question: "How does your wife feel about you being named the Sexiest Politician Alive?" That was an actual question asked of our prime minister.) It was mainly fluff, and would have remained so, except that just days earlier, London had been the target of a terrorist attack that left eleven dead and dozens more critically injured. In the UK, they were—quite literally—still sweeping up broken glass and identifying bodies when Justin appeared on *Live with Kelly and Ryan.*

When asked what Canada would do in the face of similar threats, Justin stammered that he would do "all sorts of different things," including—and I quote—"investigative national security stuff." He also said Canadians were able to handle "bad things happening without falling into a bad space." (The *dude* at the end was left unsaid, but implied.) Sleep well, Canada! Justin is on the case!

"Investigative national security stuff."

Justin Trudeau listing Canada's most pressing needs in the face of recent terrorist attacks around the world.

*T*hen there was that time he compared ISIS terrorists to Italian immigrants of the 1950s.

This one is weird, even by Justin Trudeau's standards. At a town hall meeting, our prime minister compared returning ISIS terrorist suspects to hard-working but misunderstood Italian and Portuguese immigrants. It was very bizarre.

The context: Public safety minister Ralph Goodale had recently admitted that some 250 people with links to Canada were suspected of travelling overseas to engage in terrorist activities, including at least sixty known ISIS fighters who had already returned. An understandable security concern, no?

At the town hall meeting, the father of a young daughter asked Justin how his government was going to protect Canadians from this. Justin, however, answered him by going on and on about not terrorists or security, but *cultural diversity*, about the Vietnamese boat people of the 1970s and the Portuguese and Italian newcomers of the 1950s. And no, I am not making any of this up.

Again, the question was *not* about welcoming refugees or new immigrants into Canada, it was *specifically* about terrorism. Let me repeat that: the question had nothing to do with immigration, it was about ISIS. (You remember ISIS. They're the ones who behead prisoners and throw homosexuals off rooftops.) The following is just part of Justin's rambling non-answer. Justin Trudeau, intellectual *par excellence*!

"Well, I can tell you when Italian families settled in Montreal in the postwar years, they faced terrible discrimination and people who pushed back at them and said, 'No, no, no, you don't belong here, you don't speak English or French.' Every wave of immigration has faced push-back, because of how they dressed or how they sounded or what their belief was or what their religion was."

You see? ISIS is just misunderstood is all. Like Italians.

*F*urther silly questions from those silly reporters. Consider the following exchange between Terry Milewski of the CBC and Justin Trudeau on matters of national security. Terry Milewski asked:

"If you don't want to bomb a group as ghastly as ISIS, when would you ever support real military action?"

To which Justin said, with a small, patronizing smile:

....

"Terry, Terry, that's a nonsensical question."

HANDY TIP #72 **FOR ASPIRING POLITICIANS**

When someone asks you a question you can't answer, just say that the question was "nonsensical." Here are some examples of possible usage:

Q: How do massive deficits 200 per cent greater than promised help infrastructure?

A: That's a nonsensical question.

Q: And where is all that infrastructure you promised, anyway?

A: Totally nonsensical.

Q: The inquiry into missing and murdered Aboriginal women was a multi-million-dollar fiasco that resolved nothing. Meanwhile, First Nations are without clean drinking water. What the hell?

A: That, too, is a nonsensical question.

Do you see how easy it is?

"There is no question that this happened because there is someone who feels completely excluded . . ."

*I*n 2013, a pair of bombs exploded near the finish line of the Boston Marathon, injuring hundreds, maiming many, and killing three. In an interview just *two hours* after the attack (!)—before any of the facts were known and *while the bodies were still warm*—Justin Trudeau mused on the motives behind it.

Of course, as it came out later, the Boston Marathon terrorist attack didn't occur because someone felt left out. The bombs were built and planted by a pair of Chechen brothers who had been welcomed into the United States with their families as asylum seekers. (The brothers were later connected to a brutal triple homicide two years earlier in which the victims were all but beheaded.)

The violence in Boston was ideologically driven by political extremism. It had nothing to do with someone feeling "excluded." (Justin went on to say that these poor, excluded people were "at war with innocence," whatever the hell that means.) If only we'd hugged them more! It was prime Justin Trudeau: a leadership style that is vague and feel good, with little connection to the real world. You'd almost think he grew up in a bubble or something.

MOUNTAIN EQUIPMENT **CO-OP TO THE RESCUE!**

··

"There's a lot of people, refugees, displaced peoples, fleeing violence who are facing a very, very cold winter in the mountains. Something Canada has expertise on is how to face a winter in the mountains with the right kind of equipment."

In lieu of military aid in the fight against ISIS, Justin recommended Canada share tips on how to stay warm in the mountains—with the right kind of equipment, of course! As reporter Josh Skurnik put it, "Never mind airstrikes. Victims of ISIS just need warm cocoa and woolen toques."

Whirled Affairs

RUSSIA / UKRAINE / JUSTIN / JOKE.

Talk about your awkward moments. In 2014, Russia launched an invasion of the Ukraine just days after the Sochi Winter Olympics ended. Snipers were firing on protestors in Kiev. Bodies were lying in the streets. And on what was the bloodiest day of the invasion so far, Justin Trudeau appeared on the popular current affairs program *Tout le monde en parle.*

As they discussed the violence in the Ukraine, Justin decided this was the perfect time to make a joke about the fact that Canada had recently beat Russia in hockey. "They're gonna be in a bad mood!" he chirped, clearly pleased with himself for being so witty.

What followed is excruciating to watch. The host all but glares at him, asking, "Just because of hockey?" Justin stammered that he was trying to "add some levity." At which point, one of the other panellists cut in, reminding Justin just how serious the situation in the Ukraine was. "It could turn into a massacre," he warned. And it did. The ambassador from the Ukraine didn't think Justin's comments were particularly funny either. He would later demand, and receive, an apology.

As it turns out, Justin was only warming up. Justin Trudeau, *diplomat extra-ordinaire*!

"It's very worrisome, especially because Russia lost at hockey. They will be in a bad mood!"

Justin Trudeau on the subtle nuances of geopolitical power.

Oh, those wacky, dead Ukrainians!

"There's a level of admiration I actually have for China because their basic dictatorship is allowing them to actually turn their economy around on a dime and say we need to go greenest fastest, we need to start, you know, investing in solar."

OH, **JUSTIN.**

Where to start, where to start? Human rights? Political oppression? The torture and execution of political dissenters? Tibet? The fact that China has propped up North Korea for decades? Justin seems to be under the impression that the Chinese dictatorship is a benevolent green steward. So how about this: just a few years later, the environmental watchdog Global Carbon Project reports that we will actually see an *increase* in emissions in China, not a decrease, leading to a new all-time global high.

Then there's this, from a new report by Greenpeace and the staunchly *pro*-socialist organization the Socialist Project detailing China's "unprecedented environmental crisis":

> Chinese cities are blanketed by thick smog, and images of people wearing masks or respirators are common. Only 1 per cent of China's urban population breathe air considered safe by European Union standards. The consequences are real with a million people dying every year in China as a result of air pollution . . . Some cities have managed to reduce air pollution but this is often only through moving dirty industry away from urban areas . . . A September 2017 report by Greenpeace East Asia showed that millions of Chinese people use water that isn't safe to drink . . . Coal plants and mining consume billions of cubic metres of water, leading to shortages downstream . . . Between 2011 and 2013, according to the historian Vaclav Smil, China poured more concrete than the US did in the entire 20th century.

So how's all that amazing solar energy going, Justin?

*W*hen Justin Trudeau "let out his inner Sarah Palin" (as Thomas Mulcair put it) and voiced his admiration for China's "basic dictatorship"—at a frothy Ladies Only Night, no less—the Chinese Canadian community was not impressed.

The Canadian Federation for a Democratic China, an organization that has been fighting for democracy in China for years, with many of its members having been imprisoned and tortured for speaking out against the Chinese government, described Justin's comments as "foolish." With considerable understatement, they also pointed out (to no one's real surprise), "It seems to be that he's not well-informed."

Bonus alternate history: Imagine if our boy Justin was around back in the days of Stalin or Mao. Think how he would have spun that!

There's actually a level of admiration I have for the Soviet Union, because their basic dictatorship is allowing them to collectivize their farms on a dime. Plus they're doing a great job of convincing people to relocate to Siberia. I mean, there are like trains full of people heading to the gulags, which I assume is some sort of resort. And over in China, Mao has been able to make a great leap forward without forcing millions into starvation—as far as I know.

Namaste, Yo!

JUSTIN'S EXCELLENT **INDIAN ADVENTURE.**

Justin's unintentionally hilarious 2018 trip to India featured lots of Mr. Dress-up moments and Bollywood dance moves. What it didn't offer was much in the way of substance. But that's okay, because the rest of the world simply *loves* Justin!! Right? Maybe not . . .

*I*n the *Washington Post*, respected Indian journalist Barkha Dutt wrote about Justin's romp through India, noting that the Canadian prime minister came across as "silly, diminished and desperate" on his visit.

> Flighty and facetious. His orchestrated dance moves and multiple costume changes in heavily embroidered kurtas and sherwanis make him look more like an actor on a movie set or a guest at a wedding than a politician who is here to talk business. Suddenly, all that charisma and cuteness seem constructed, manufactured and, above all, not serious.

On watching Justin "sashaying out, doing the Bhangra dance," she adds: "You could feel the collective groan of Indians: *Please. Stop. Enough Already.*" Or, as one official in the Indian government put it: "He seems . . . much more convinced of his own rock-star status than we ever were."

The lesson in all of this? Turns out, the rest of the world may not be quite as enamoured with ol' Justin as we seem to think they are.

"Our countries both marked some big milestones. You celebrated the 70th Anniversary of Indian Independence, and we celebrated the 100th Anniversary of Canadian Confederation!"

At a state event in India, Justin Trudeau honours Canada 150 in his own inimitable way.

**CANADIAN PRIME MINISTER JUSTIN TRUDEAU'S VISIT
WAS A DISASTER THAT HAS LITTLE PARALLEL
IN INDIA'S RECENT DIPLOMATIC HISTORY**

Times of India

●

INDIA TRIP RAISES EYEBROWS

Hindustan Times

●

TOO FLASHY EVEN FOR AN INDIAN?

Outlook

●

**JUSTIN TRUDEAU'S BHANGRA TO PEPPY BEATS OF THE DHOL
IN CANADA HOUSE IN DELHI HAS LEFT MANY UNIMPRESSED. NOT
JUST CANADIANS WHO THOUGHT IT WAS "EMBARRASSING"
BUT EVEN INDIANS WERE UNHAPPY**

New Indian Express

●

TRUDEAU SHOOTS HIMSELF IN THE FOOT ONCE AGAIN

New Indian Express

●

"Over a billion dollars of investment *in Canada*."

Emphasis his.

Hooray!

After an eight-day, $1.5 *million* jaunt in India with his wife and kids, Justin spent all of one (count 'em, one!) afternoon meeting with Indian businessmen. He then went home and trumpeted his achievements: a billion dollars of investment in Canada. Take that people who say he was using his trip to India as an expensive, publicly funded photo op!

Except . . . (and you just knew there was going to be an "except," didn't you?) that billion-dollar investment package he was bragging about? Turns out, *only $250 million* of it was in Canada. The rest was invested in India.

POP QUIZ

Is one billion dollars MORE or LESS than 250 million?

Answer: Well, it depends if you're relying on a former substitute teacher to manage a G7 economy. Because those guys have their own crazy approach to math that is beyond such concepts as time and space!

MR. DRESS-UP 2.0

There's nothing Justin enjoys more than dressing up. You'd almost think he was a former drama teacher or something.

Promises, Promises,

PINOCCHIO **2.0.**

When Justin Trudeau reneged on his promise to bring in electoral reform, the NDP's Nathan Cullen, usually a fairly affable soul, fumed, "What Trudeau proved himself [to be] today was . . . a liar, of the most cynical variety of politician."

I'll admit, I kinda like Nathan Cullen. He has a habit of cutting to the heart of the matter. He's intelligent, funny, articulate, and bald. Sort of the anti–Justin Trudeau. (If you look up Justin in the dictionary, it says: "Opposite: *See* Nathan Cullen.")

But come on. Just because someone says one thing and does another doesn't mean they're lying. It may be that their *idea* of what is true has changed. Similarly, the fact that a politician pulls the plug on something just because he realizes that he's not going to be able to stack the results in his favour doesn't make him a cynical, garden-variety politician. Oh, wait . . . it totally does. Carry on, then.

"2015 will be the last federal election conducted under the first-past-the-post voting system!"

And you know it's true because it was part of the official Liberal Party platform *and* the Speech from the Throne!

*B*reaking news! Child of privilege takes bold stance: "That's not the way I was raised!"

....

"Canadians elect governments to do hard things and don't expect us to throw up our hands when things are a little difficult . . . 'Oh, it's more difficult than we thought it could be and therefore we're just going to give up.' No, I'm sorry, that's not the way I was raised."

Justin Trudeau displaying his steely resolve. He was referring *specifically* to electoral reform and his promise to end our current first-past-the-post system. That was in December 2016. Two months later, he decided it was, in fact, too much work, and he boldly gave up. In the words of Monty Python, he bravely buggered off.

DECEMBER 2, 2016

TRUDEAU INSISTS ELECTION REFORM STILL ON TABLE

Toronto Star

•

FEBRUARY 1, 2017

TRUDEAU ABANDONS PLEDGE TO REFORM CANADA'S ELECTIONS

Toronto Star

•

*S*o why did Justin abandon his promise so readily? Let us harken back to those Dark Days of 2011, when Stephen Harper, The Most Evil Man Who Has Ever Lived™, *stole* the Canadian election, taking a majority government with a mere 39 per cent of the vote! You may recall the anger, the protests, the signs declaring "I am part of the 60 per cent"!

Thank goodness those days are over! Compare this to the sunny ways of 2015, when Justin Trudeau's Liberals won a strong and completely legitimate mandate from the Canadian people, garnering an even larger majority than Harper did with a resounding . . . 39 per cent of the vote.

You may not recall the angry protests or media-fed outrage after Justin's win, because there were none.

Under Canada's first-past-the-post system, a candidate doesn't need an outright majority of votes to win their riding, they just need to win the most votes among competing candidates. This system rewards parties like the Liberals and Conservatives, who are routinely overrepresented in Parliament, while severely *under*representing parties like the NDP and the Green.

Back when the Liberals were in third place, Justin thought this was outrageous! (Because at that time it was the Liberals who were severely underrepresented.) He vowed to end this once and for all!

But then he got elected . . . and the system was now *benefiting* the Liberals, who received an even greater majority than Harper did with the same per cent of the vote. Suddenly, it didn't seem so bad.

$\mathcal{S}$o what are the options? If you want to reform our voting system, the solution seems fairly obvious: a party that gets 12 per cent of the vote should get 12 per cent of the seats, a party that gets 39 per cent of the vote, as the Liberals did, should get 39 per cent of the seats. And so on.

Unfortunately for Justin, this would hamper the Liberals while *helping* the NDP. (Our current government, for example, would *not* be a Liberal majority. It would be a minority government with the NDP holding the balance of power.)

Instead of proportional representation, Justin favoured a "ranked ballot," which no one has ever asked for—ever. Under this system, voters would be required to rate their choices from first to third. Elections Canada would then tally these up accordingly, because you are always hearing people say, "What really matters to me is that my *second choice* gets elected, even if the candidate I voted for got more votes in the first round."

A "ranked ballot" system would, of course, keep the Liberals in power indefinitely. The Liberals, after all, are everyone's *second* choice. No self-respecting NDPer would list the Conservatives as their second choice, any more than a Conservative voter would list the NDP as theirs. It was designed to keep the Liberals in government forever.

When it became clear that Justin was not going to get the results he wanted, he simply pulled the plug on the entire process without even bringing forward a vote in the House. As Andrew Coyne noted, Trudeau was fully prepared to accept his *own* proposal. Just not other people's proposals.

JUSTIN TRUDEAU: **MY WORD IS MY BOND!**

"I make promises because I believe in them."

Justin Trudeau, promise-keeper!

*J*ustin Trudeau *Before* the Election and Justin Trudeau *After* the Election: Can You Spot the Difference?

"As far as Canada Post, we commit to restore door-to-door home delivery."

Justin Trudeau on the campaign trail.

"Those households that were converted during the past government's tenure will not be returned to home door-to-door delivery."

Once in office, Justin Trudeau's public services minister announced that the 840,000 households across Canada that had lost home mail delivery will not have door-to-door delivery restored.

Suckers!

"No veteran will be forced to fight their own government for the support and compensation that they have earned . . . We will reinstate lifelong pensions and increase their value in line with the obligation we have made to those injured in the line of duty."

"Why are we still fighting against certain veterans' groups in court? Because they are asking for more than we are able to give."

The prime minister tells a wounded Canadian war vet that there's just not enough to go around. Seems cold-hearted, but come on, it's not like Justin *campaigned* on reinstating cuts to military pensions, right? Oh wait. He totally did.

Even after taking the government to court and even after the Liberals caved, the amounts offered were still inadequate to Canada's veterans. But so what, right? We have to cut corners somewhere, after all! Those $8.1 million outdoor skating rinks on Parliament Hill aren't going to pay for themselves!

"We will make free votes in the House of Commons standard practice."

Justin's campaign platform during the 2015 election.

OCTOBER 5, 2017

MP KICKED OFF TWO COMMITTEES FOR BREAKING LIBERAL RANKS ON TAX CHANGES

CBC News

I'll take "Reality versus Rhetoric" for 200 points, Alex!

*A*t this point, you may be beginning to suspect that the Liberal Party of Canada will say absolutely anything to get elected, that they will promise one thing in one part of the country and promise something completely different in another part. But that's not true! It's just that, when you're Justin Trudeau throwing promises around like confetti at a parade, with so many goodies to so many people, it's hard not to get caught up in the euphoria of it all. Happens to the best of us. Case in point, the following two statements made in two different parts of the country only a few months apart.

For those of you who thought you were voting *in favour* of pipelines: wrong! And for those of you who thought you were voting *against* pipelines: wrong again! It's not a contradiction; it's a Zenlike paradox. Remember: we have to rethink such basic concepts as time and space, to say nothing of truth and duplicity.

"I am very much in favour of the west/east pipeline."

Justin Trudeau, speaking in Alberta, April 2014.

"Energy East's pipeline project does not have the necessary 'social license' required."

Justin Trudeau, speaking in Quebec, December 2014.

"You cannot play favourites. You can't pander to votes in the east by attacking the west, or vice versa . . . To try and subdivide and strategically map out who you want to speak to and who you're going to ignore is exactly *not* what the Liberal Party is gonna do."

Justin Trudeau, speaking in English.

"Canada isn't doing well . . . because it's Albertans who control our collective socio-democratic agenda."

Justin Trudeau, speaking in French.

*I*nterviewed in Quebec before he became prime minister, Justin answered the following question . . .

"Is Canada better served when there are more Quebecers in power than more Albertans in power?"

. . . in the following manner:

....

"I am Liberal, therefore of course I think that the answer is yes. Certainly, when we look at the great Prime Ministers of the 20th century, the only ones that have held up are MPs from Quebec. We have a role. This country, Canada, is ours."

Because pandering to regional divisions is "exactly *not* what the Liberal Party is gonna do"!

The only thing to add, I suppose, is: Great prime ministers of the twentieth century? Paul Martin? Really?

POP QUIZ: **BONUS QUESTION**

Remember when Justin announced that all Liberal senators would henceforth be considered independent and would no longer have to vote along party lines? Turns out that Justin's subsequent, supposedly "independent" appointees voted along Liberal party lines 94.5 per cent of the time. Funny, that.

Question: Is slavishly toeing the party line 94.5 per cent of the time "independent"?

Sunny Ways!

JUSTIN "TRANSPARENCY-IS-MY-MIDDLE-NAME" TRUDEAU

Justin Trudeau came to power promising a new era of honesty, openness, and respect for Parliament. Let's see how that played out, shall we?

"We . . . made a commitment to bring new leadership and a new tone to Ottawa . . . We will not let you down!"

Wait for it, wait for it . . .

JUSTIN TAKES THE HIGH ROAD!

"It is not my practice and it is not, I think, helpful to make personal attacks or to denigrate an individual."

Justin Trudeau on the importance of decorum during political discourse.

"You are a piece of sh*t!"

Justin Trudeau maintaining proper decorum while addressing a member of another party in the House of Commons.

I'm sure he meant it in a nice way . . .

"Sunny ways, my friends! Sunny ways."

Justin Trudeau promises a new era!

"The challenge that I have is to get Canadians to move away from 'Oh, look at that fellow in his undershirt. He mustn't have much judgement,' to, 'Oh, look at Mr. Harper raising taxes on tricycles and baby clothes. *He* must have very poor judgement.' And I do that in a way that is positive, not negative."

Because accusing your opponent of taking money from babies is not negative when Justin does it! Sunny ways, my friends!

"We didn't join them in the gutter."

Justin Trudeau at the 2018 Liberal Convention, boasting about how the Liberals took the high road.

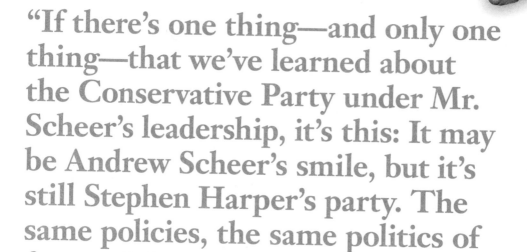

"If there's one thing—and only one thing—that we've learned about the Conservative Party under Mr. Scheer's leadership, it's this: It may be Andrew Scheer's smile, but it's still Stephen Harper's party. The same policies, the same politics of fear and division."

Justin—in the very same speech!—just moments after preaching, yet again, about "sunny ways."

He also said, "It is easy to give into cynicism when it comes to politics." Gosh, I wonder why . . .

So how does Justin's patented Sunny Ways stack up against the Dark Ages of Stephen Harper? Let's ask someone who doesn't have a dog in the fight, someone who is neither Liberal nor Conservative: Thomas Mulcair, a fine man who served as the leader of the NDP under both the Harper and Trudeau governments.

The Liberals have veered radically to the left under Justin Trudeau, so one would imagine that Justin would be more considerate to the NDP than the Conservatives had been. Turns out, no.

"I found Harper more respectful of me as a leader in Parliament than I find Mr. Trudeau."

Thomas Mulcair, who knows Justin firsthand.

MAKE BETTER CHOICES, PEOPLE!!

"When you put a price on things you don't want, which is pollution, you encourage people to make better choices."

Justin Trudeau explaining how soaring gas prices in BC were a good thing.

Fair enough. Carbon taxes and higher gas prices will force families to make "better choices" about consuming fuel, wasting resources, limiting carbon dioxide emissions, etc.

For example . . .

TRUDEAU FAMILY GETTING ITS MEALS DELIVERED FROM 24 SUSSEX TO RIDEAU COTTAGE

CBC News

•

This news broke just three days after Justin told Canadians that higher gas prices would lead to "better choices."

The CBC story goes on to say:

> Even though no one has called 24 Sussex Drive home for more than two years, staff have been using the kitchen there to prepare meals for the Trudeau family, which are then ferried across the way to Rideau Cottage.

That's right. His meals are being prepared and then driven down the road every day, less than a kilometre away. (24 Sussex is under renovation, but Rideau Cottage is a beautiful building and, presumably, has a kitchen of its own.) Better choices, people! We got a planet to save!

For those keeping score, this is at least, oh, half-a-dozen "Do as I say, not as I do" lessons from Justin.

PLEASE NOTE: As per actual legal advice, I am required to inform any readers too dense to figure it out on their own that the estimate of "half-a-dozen" or so "do as I say" moments is a rhetorical device and is not in any way meant to suggest that there are, or were, exactly that many such moments. Thank you.

*U*nder the cruel regime of The Evil Stephen Harper, The World's Most Vile Human Being™, the media often complained about limited access. Why? Because Harper was a DICTATOR, that's WHY! And not one of those good dictators like in China, but a horrible, Conservative dictator!

This would all change under Justin. And it did, though not quite in the way we imagined.

SEPTEMBER 27, 2017

CANADA'S ACCESS-TO-INFORMATION SYSTEM HAS WORSENED UNDER TRUDEAU GOVERNMENT

Globe and Mail

•

That was just two years into his mandate. He works fast, this kid.

As Laura Stone reported in the *Globe and Mail*, a freedom-of-information audit by News Media Canada, a national association representing Canadian news media, gave the Liberals a failing grade on disclosure of information. It was, the audit noted, "even worse than in the latter years of the former Stephen Harper government."

More worrisome still were provisions brought forward by the Liberals that would have allowed access-to-information requests to be rejected based solely on their size, scope, or if they were considered "vexatious." As Nathan Cullen put it, "It's got to be a bad day for Liberals when Stephen Harper was more open to the Canadian public than they are."

Woke Bae

JUSTIN TRUDEAU: SUPER-DUPER FEMINIST!

We know that Justin Trudeau is a feminist because he tells us. Repeatedly. Not only that, but he has always been very, very, very respectful of women's personal space. We know that, too, because he told us so. It's right out of Leacock: *Jean-Pierre is the bravest man in France: he told us, and he should know.*

Likewise, Justin Trudeau is also the most woke man in Canada: he told us, and he should know! (Justin loves to toot his own horn in these matters.) He even dreams of a time when a woman might someday become prime minister . . .

"Peoplekind."

Justin Trudeau correcting a woman's use of the word "mankind."

Also verboten, apparently:

hu*man*
fe*male*
per*son*

Because purging the English language of unacceptable syntax and grammatical roots is a matter of urgent political concern!

Please note, also deemed problematic are the following surnames: John*son*, Swan*son*, Han*son*, Ol*son*, Wil*son*, Robert*son*, Robin*son*, Donald*son*, David*son*, Ander*son*, Thomp*son*, Jack*son*, etcetera. And don't get me started on names like A*man*da and *Man*di!

*M*ANSPLAINING 101: When Justin used the word *peoplekind* at a town hall meeting in Edmonton, media around the world, from the BBC to CNN, laughed at him. Scrambling to avoid further ridicule, he claimed he was only "joking." But if you watch the clip, easily found on YouTube, it's painfully clear that he was *not* joking. Not in the least. He has a smug smile, but that doesn't make it a joke.

TO RECAP: Justin Trudeau (a) *interrupts* a woman to (b) mansplain the proper use of pronouns to her. Here is a transcript of the key moment in that exchange:

Young woman asking about government policies regarding charities:

"Maternal love is the love that is going to change the future of mankind, so we'd like you to—"

Justin Trudeau (cutting her off; note the use of the Royal "We"):

"We like to say *peoplekind*, not necessarily *mankind*. It's more inclusive."

Pander much?

"There's lots of things you can do to be a better feminist as a man, but here's a simple one: don't interrupt women."

Justin Trudeau mansplains feminism to men (in a Snapchat selfie, no less!).

If only he took that advice himself!

YOUR WORST THEN HITTLER!!!

Justin's "peoplekind" comment quickly went viral and was roundly mocked both at home and abroad. In response, Justin's old college buddy—and, until recently, key inner circle adviser in the PMO—Gerald Butts (he of the $126,000 moving expenses) flew into a spittle-flecked Twitter rage, denouncing anyone who would dare "torque" the prime minister's words as being in league with "alt-right nazis."

That's right, children! If your prime minister says something dumb, and you laugh at him, you're a nazi. One mustn't mock Our Glorious Leader.

You think I'm kidding about the Liberal government policing language, but consider this: In 2018, Service Canada instructed its employees to stop using gender-specific terms when dealing with the public. These included such incendiary and offensive words as—and no, I'm not making any of this up—*mother*, *father*, *Mr.*, and *Ms.*

That's right, *Ms.* is now unacceptable. *O brave new world . . . !*

On applying the same rules to everyone: Justin fired MP Kent Hehr from his cabinet for invading female colleagues' personal space with his wheelchair (Hehr is paraplegic) and for referring to a female member of staff as "yummy." Fair enough. Here is Justin laying down the law in a 2018 interview with the CBC:

> REPORTER: Will the same standard apply to you if someone comes forward?
>
> JUSTIN: The standard applies to everyone. There is no context in which someone doesn't have responsibility for things they have done in the past.

Later in that same interview:

> REPORTER: You've mentioned the past. Some of the cases we've heard from so far date far back, into the years. And I'm wondering, as you look back at your own career, is there a chance at some point that your actions might have not been construed the way they were intended?
>
> JUSTIN: I don't think so. I've been very, very careful all my life to be thoughtful, to be respectful of people's space.

Good to know!

"I've been working on issues around sexual assault for over 25 years. My first activism and engagement was at the sexual assault centre at McGill students' society where I was one of the first male facilitators in their outreach program leading conversations—sometimes very difficult ones—on the issues of consent, communications, accountability, power dynamics."

How to be an ally, Justin edition! He's been woke for twenty-five years! He's been aware of "issues of consent" and "power dynamics" for twenty-five years as well. That's terrific. Except . . .

BREAKING NEWS! JUSTIN GETS ALL HANDSY: "IF I HAD KNOWN YOU MATTERED, I WOULDN'T HAVE DONE IT!"

Given Justin's self-congratulatory proclamations about how sensitive and thoughtful he is (again, Justin Trudeau's favourite topic is always Justin Trudeau), what are we to make of an incident that purportedly occurred when he was just a callow youth of twenty-eight who didn't know any better? In 2000, Justin—already a celebrity—was publicly accused of groping and inappropriately "handling" a woman he *thought* was just a local reporter. In fact, she was also on assignment for both the *National Post* and *Vancouver Sun*. The account of the incident that followed was scathing:

> It's not a rare incident to have a young reporter, especially a female who is working for a small community newspaper, be considered an underling to their "more predominant" associates and blatantly disrespected because of it. But shouldn't the son of a former prime minister be aware of the rights and wrongs that go along with public socializing? Didn't he learn, through his vast experiences in public life, that groping a strange young woman isn't in the handbook of proper etiquette, regardless of who she is . . . ?
>
> *Creston Valley Advance*, August 14, 2000

"I'm sorry. If I had known you were reporting for a national paper, I never would have been so forward."

Justin's oddly worded "apology" to a young female reporter following a raucous summer beer festival in Creston, BC.

He would later say there was no need for an investigation into his behaviour because "people experience things differently." Adding, "Who knows where her mind was?" So there you go, ladies. You just experience things "differently," that's all.

Note to self: Look up *gaslighting*, symptoms of.

*J*ustin's defence—*Had I known you mattered and had a national voice, I would never have done it*—seems a bit creepy, no? The editor and the newspaper stand by the story. The young woman in question was reportedly distressed after the incident.

Fallout? Not a damn thing. As it turns out, zero tolerance is zero tolerance, except when it comes to Justin. As for the desperate excuse floated by his supporters—that this was all "eighteen years ago" and thus doesn't matter—please see the previous pages, where he boasts about his *twenty-five years* of wokeness.

Here, lemme just fix that earlier quote: There's lots of things you can do to be a better feminist as a man, but here's a simple one: "don't grope women."

HISTORY **LESSONS**

"If you had to predict, and say 'One of my three kids will be prime minister,' which one would you put your money on?"

"I will say, I have one daughter, and there is something very special about imagining a woman prime minister. I think it's long overdue. I just don't think we have to wait that long. I think it should be sooner than that."

Justin Trudeau being interviewed in 2017.

Because a woman prime minister is long overdue!

The Right Honourable
Kim Campbell, prime
minister of Canada, 1993.

GREAT MOMENTS IN CANADIAN POLITICAL ORATORY #2

Who Said It: Wilfrid Laurier or Justin Trudeau?

"Canada has become a star to which is directed the gaze of the whole civilized world. That is what we have done."

or . . .

"I look at what I have as a challenge and I could list a whole bunch of different challenges, and I choose not to be daunted by any of them."

Our Home on Native Land

JUSTIN TRUDEAU: ALLY!

*H*ave you seen that cool Indigenous tattoo Justin Trudeau has on his shoulder of a thunderbird, which is totally *not* cultural appropriation? Why not? Because it's Justin! He has a special relationship with Indigenous peoples in Canada! We know this because he told us. Yay Justin! But don't just take his word for it. Consider the following question posed in the House of Commons by Cree member of Parliament Romeo Saganash:

> **"WHY DOESN'T THE PRIME MINISTER JUST SAY THE TRUTH AND TELL THE INDIGENOUS PEOPLES THAT HE DOESN'T GIVE A F*CK ABOUT THEIR RIGHTS."**

Um . . . Okay. So maybe that's not the best example. The MP in question would later withdraw the use of the f-bomb but not the sentiment behind it.

"A place to store their canoes."

Land of the Silver Birch. Justin Trudeau discusses the most pressing needs facing young Indigenous people in Canada today.

*F*un things happen when Justin goes off script! It's like watching a junior high volleyball game: once that ball goes over the net, you have no idea where it's going to go next. It could go up, could go down, could veer wildly to the left or right, or even hit the ceiling as players scramble about in all directions.

Here's our Justin, speaking freely and unscripted—off-the-cuff and from the heart!—at a town hall meeting in Saskatoon, where he was asked about the challenges facing Indigenous youth. He talked about canoe sheds (see previous page), but the full quote is even better. He went *full* Justin on us. A virtuoso performance!

In the transcript that follows, please note (a) the patronizing manner in which he dismisses Indigenous chiefs (those chiefs, what the hell do they know?), (b) his own inflated claims of having a more authentic connection to young people than they do, and (c) the hilarious finale, where he throws in Wi-Fi access. Because, when you're Justin Trudeau trying to imagine the challenges facing underprivileged members of society, the best you can come up with is a place to park your boat and better Wi-Fi.

An Indigenous MP later complained that Justin's comments were "borderline racist." But one shouldn't ascribe to racism what can adequately be explained by a puffed-up sense of entitlement. (Note to self: Look up *privilege*, poster boy of.)

"I've spoken with a number of chiefs who said, 'Y'know, we need a youth centre in our community.' Okay, well, what do you want in that youth centre? 'Well, you know, we need TVs and lounges and sofas so they can hang around.' And when a chief says that to me, I pretty much know they haven't actually talked to their young people. Because most of the young people I've talked to are asking for a place to store their canoes and paddles so they can connect back out on the land, and a place with internet access so that they can do their homework in a meaningful way, because their homes are often too crowded."

Justin Trudeau, on a roll.

"A sacred obligation."

Justin Trudeau on the responsibilities of the federal government toward Indigenous peoples in Canada.

Except . . .

CANADA HAS SPENT $110,000 TO AVOID PAYING $6,000 FOR INDIGENOUS TEEN'S ORTHODONTICS

The Guardian

•

The article begins:

> Days after Justin Trudeau told the United Nations that his government was working hard to improve the quality of life for indigenous peoples in Canada, it has emerged that his government spent more than C$110,000 . . . in legal fees to avoid spending C$6,000 on orthodontics for a First Nations teenager suffering from chronic pain.

The girl in question, from the Sucker Creek First Nation, suffered from severe pain and migraines stemming from an impacted tooth and a serious overbite. Without surgery, she could have trouble eating and even speaking.

One doesn't want to set a precedent, though. Which is why the Liberal government of Canada spent more money on legal fees *fighting* her request than simply paying for the damned surgery.

We gotta cut costs somewhere, right? Those $8.1 million outdoor skating rinks on Parliament Hill don't pay for themselves, bucko!

*I*n 2012, Justin Trudeau challenged the Conservatives to a charity boxing match. His opponent was a young but troubled senator, Patrick Brazeau, of the Anishinabe First Nation.

Justin won the match, after which he symbolically cut off some of the senator's ponytail (just in case losing a boxing match on national television wasn't emasculating enough to a Native male).

"I said, we're both known for our long hair . . . let's say the loser gets a haircut. He resisted back a little bit, pointing out that hair has a cultural significance for First Nations peoples. I said, I know. That's why I proposed it. When a warrior cuts his hair it's a sign of shame."

"It wasn't random. I wanted someone who would be a good foil, and we stumbled upon the scrappy tough-guy senator from an indigenous community. He fit the bill, and it was a very nice counterpoint . . . I saw it as the right kind of narrative, the right story to tell."

You would think that winning the boxing match and humiliating his opponent would be enough, but no. Justin—being Justin—couldn't resist crowing about it to *Rolling Stone* magazine, bragging aboout how he intentionally chose a First Nations opponent. *Rolling Stone* compared his comments to "a CFO in a company-budget markup session," which is to say, calculated, contrived, and slightly unsettling. *The right kind of narrative.*

Justin, channeling his inner warrior. Check out that cool thunderbird tat! Remember, it's not appropriation when Justin does it.

"Thank you very much for your donation tonight. I really appreciate it . . . Thank you, sir, for your donation to the Liberal Party of Canada. I really appreciate you being here tonight."

Cue: laughter and applause

*T*hat's nice. Justin thanking someone for donating money to the Liberal Party of Canada. Nothing smarmy or smug about *that*, right?

Some context: The Grassy Narrows First Nations have suffered from the environmental impact and aftermath of mercury poisoning for decades. It's an ongoing national disgrace, something Justin promised to address. But of course he didn't.

Meanwhile, at a swanky $1,500-a-plate Liberal fundraiser in Toronto, a protestor paid to attend in order to ask Justin about this. As he took the stage, this is what she said:

"PRIME MINISTER TRUDEAU, PEOPLE AT GRASSY NARROWS ARE SUFFERING FROM MERCURY POISONING. YOU COMMITTED TO ADDRESSING THIS CRISIS. WHEN WILL YOU KEEP THAT PROMISE?"

That last part was shouted as she was strong-armed out of the room by security.

Justin's response? He mugged to the crowd, saying, smugly, "Thank you very much for your donation tonight," as the crowd hooted and laughed.

An Indigenous man in the audience then shouted, "If your family was suffering from mercury poisoning, what would you do? If it was your family, would you accept it?"

He too was hustled out the door. Egged on by the crowd, Justin again mocked the protestors, saying, "Thank you, sir, for your donation to the Liberal Party of Canada. I really appreciate you being here." This was met by more laughter and applause.

Y'know, every now and then, the mask slips . . .

*W*hen Justin was caught on tape mocking an Indigenous woman at a Liberal fundraiser, Grand Chief Stewart Phillip was not impressed. He went on national TV and said that Justin's actions had revealed the prime minister's true character, one that was smarmy and mean-spirited, arrogant and self-centered. The Grand Chief went on to remind Canadians of the scope of the tragedy in Grassy Narrows, where people live with the legacy of mercury poisoning. He was especially disappointed with the way Liberal Party members in the room applauded Justin when he insulted the protesters. It was, the chief felt, indicative of a long-standing sense of entitlement entrenched in the Liberal Party of Canada.

But check out Justin's cool tattoo! It has a thunderbird and everything! If that doesn't prove how much he simply LOVES our First Nations peoples nothing will. Right?

Justin & the Media: A Love Story

JUSTIN KNOWS HOW TO WOO THE MEDIA
AND THE MEDIA LOVES TO BE WOOED.

In the midst of the 2015 election, Justin suddenly announced he would be giving the CBC a $150 million boost in funding. Some more cynical than I might suggest that $150 million buys you a lot of good coverage, but not me! (Is it impolite to point out that the CBC's lead anchor at the time, Peter Mansbridge, also officiated at Justin Trudeau's director of communications' wedding? Cozy, no?)

It gets better. With clockwork predictability, Justin announced in the lead-up to the 2019 election that he would be providing a further $560 million for Canadian print media. But I am sure none of that will sway Canada's unimpeachable journalists from holding Justin to account!

$\mathcal{C}$onsider the following hard-hitting question, as posed by Global News as one "the entire country wants to know":

"What shampoo do you use?"

Justin doesn't dodge *this* question! No, sir. He answers with boldness and clarity:

....

"Whatever happens to be hanging around at the time."

Teen Beat take note. *That's* how you conduct a celebrity interview!

"Our new political crush!"

The always incisive *Elle* magazine.

Elle would go on to comment, approvingly, on Justin's cute butt (really) and the fact that he was "pals with President Obama," ending their gushing fan letter with a heartfelt "thanks for being you, Justin!"

*O*kay. So the glossy magazines, American daytime TV programs, and regular broadcasters may not ask hard-hitting questions, but what about smaller, scrappier independent media? Here is a reporter from GroundWire, a national non-profit news organization, at a press conference with Justin Trudeau, prefacing what is sure to be a hard-hitting question on child tax benefits:

> Couple of praise points, obviously. First, congratulations on your Canada Day speech. Excellent oration, particularly in French, and an awesome opportunity to see you represent Gen-X to such a high capacity. Thank you so much for your great work and your team.

Canada's independent news media, ladies and gentlemen! PS: I gotta say, I love the use of *"obviously"* in the above.

*J*ustin went to China and proudly failed to get a trade deal. (Apparently, his admiration for China's basic dictatorship did not sway them, nor did his years backpacking in Asia. Go figure.) On the flight back, though, something incredible happened, even more so because it was noted only in passing.

As Steven Chase from the *Globe and Mail* reported:

> Justin Trudeau offered to talk to media on the plane home from China to give them inside scoop on his trip but only if journalists gave their solemn word not to report any of what PM told us.

Chase admits that he was tempted by Justin's offer, calling it "enticing," but in the end decided not to. Others in the press gallery were not so reticent, however, and they happily took part in a *secret* briefing. As Chase noted, it was a difficult choice "forced on us: Learn things you are forbidden to report—or walk away."

Remember when Justin criticized the Conservatives for being all secretive? Remember how he promised a new era of transparency? Glad those days are behind us! Yay journalistic integrity!

ON NOT DODGING THE ISSUES.

"Because I am a federal politician, because I want to become prime minister, I think it would be very inappropriate for me to take a firm position."

Justin at a press scrum after he was asked about his views on contentious issues. In this case, the right to die with dignity.

He was waiting for the courts to rule on it, y'see. Which is all fine and good, but what makes this interesting is the reasoning behind it: *"Because I want to be prime minister . . ."* Way to take a stance, Justin!

JUSTIN'S **TEARS.**

Justin loves to apologize for things he had nothing to do with. These are often worthy causes and past wrongs, but what's really strange is how much he loves to cry when the cameras are rolling. When most people cry, they quickly try to wipe away their tears. But not our Justin. He just stands there with tears streaming down his face. Weird, right? That's not how normal people cry. Again, you'd almost think he was a former drama teacher.

How normal people cry

How Justin Trudeau cries

𝔐aybe the media isn't quite as enamoured with Justin as Justin seems to think they are. *Here I am photo-bombing a wedding! Here I am jogging topless through Stanley Park! Quick, take my picture!* TAKE MY PICTURE! *Ain't I just adorable!!!* Consider the following from across the political spectrum:

IF TRUDEAU IS THE FREE WORLD'S LAST HOPE, THE FREE WORLD IS DOOMED.
National Post

•

But what do they know? They're just a bunch of right-wing meanies.

HE SAYS ONE THING AND THEN EITHER FORGETS HE SAID IT OR DOES SOMETHING ELSE. IT'S AS IF THE COUNTRY IS RUN BY A MAGIC 8 BALL.
Vinay Menon, *Toronto Star*

•

But what do they know? They're just a bunch of left-wing meanies.

HE DOESN'T HAVE AN INTELLECTUAL BONE IN HIS BODY. HE'S SOMEWHERE BETWEEN FLOWER POWER AND NEW AGE. HE'S OFTEN AT A LOSS FOR WORDS.
Lysiane Gagnon, *Globe and Mail*

•

But what do they know? They're just a bunch of centrist meanies.

Other People's Money

*S*iri, what is both the funniest *and* most depressing Canadian headline of the last four years?

LIBERAL SPENDING REVIEW SO FAR IDENTIFIES NO CUTS, BUT HIGHLIGHTS NEW SPENDING
Globe and Mail

•

Let's savour that for a moment, shall we? "Liberal spending review so far identifies no cuts, but instead highlights new spending." The article goes on to explain:

> A Liberal government pledge to root out waste and inefficient programs has yet to identify any spending cuts. Instead, the government is using the review to justify new spending.

You can't make this stuff up!

"The budget will balance itself . . ."

"I've committed to continuing to run balanced budgets. In fact, it is Conservatives who run deficits. Liberals balance budgets. That's what history has shown."

Justin Trudeau, making stuff up.

"I am looking straight at Canadians and being honest the way I always have. We said we are committed to balanced budgets and we are. We will balance that budget in 2019."

Justin Trudeau on the campaign trail, during the leader's debate. It was a promise "cast in stone," he said.

And you know it's true because a promise from the Liberals is something you can bank on!

But wait, the budget was already balanced when you arrived . . .

o it turns out, budgets don't balance themselves. Justin inherited a $7.5 billion *surplus* when he was first elected, but—through careful economic stewardship—in just three short years he managed to turn that into a $20 billion *deficit*. But that's okay. Because it's all about infrastructure! And about growing the economy! (Apparently, infrastructure spending grows the economy. Who knew?)

During the 2015 campaign, Justin promised that he would run "a modest short-term deficit" of less than $10 billion over the first three years, after which we would magically return to a balanced budget in 2019. (You've probably noticed all the amazing infrastructure we have now. You can't turn around in this country without running into another infrastructure success story!)

Unfortunately, Justin's carefully managed "modest" deficit quickly ballooned by 200 per cent. The 2019 budget—the year that the Liberals were going to get back to the balanced books that they inherited from the Conservatives—has a deficit of $20 billion. Or, to show that in its proper numerical form: $20,000,000,000.00.

Forget balancing the books in 2019. The timeline for eliminating the Liberal's deficit has now been pushed back to 2041. Which is to say, the budget should have balanced itself just in time for Justin's seventieth birthday party.

But who cares! We won't be the ones paying that off. It will be our kids and our kids' kids who have to pay it off. Suckers! What did our children ever do for us? Live for the moment, I say! *Carpe diem!*

*M*ore fun with numbers. In April 2019, the International Monetary Fund predicted Canada's economy would grow 1.5 per cent! Hooray! Surely the Liberals could cite this as evidence that their deficit-ridden approach was working. Except . . .

Canada's GDP: $2.1 trillion
  Federal deficit: $18.1 billion
  Provincial deficit (combined): $8.4 billion
Total deficit: $26.5 billion

Which means our *total deficit* works out to be . . . drum roll please . . . *1.2 per cent of our GDP.*

In other words, what little growth there was is effectively cancelled out by deficits. It's like taking out a huge bank loan and then swaggering about boasting of how rich you've suddenly become. *Handy tip from the Justin Trudeau School of Economics*: When the bank forecloses on your home, walk in, head held high, and say, "My bank account will balance itself!"

POP **QUIZ**

If the government spends $20 billion more than it takes in, is this "balanced"? You can take a moment to ponder that while we play the *Jeopardy!* theme song in the background . . .

"We can grow the economy not from the top down . . . but from the heart outwards!"

Care Bears to the rescue!

We will grow the economy
from the heart out . . .

A TALE OF TWO SCANDALS:

MIKE DUFFY VS. GERALD BUTTS

Let's look at two separate scandals involving expenses, shall we? See if you can spot the difference.

MIKE DUFFY

SENATE LIVING COSTS: $90,172.24

Although he'd lived in Ottawa for decades, Conservative senator Mike Duffy listed a PEI property as his primary residence. This enabled him to claim more than $90,000 in living costs over the course of four years. When news of this emerged, Prime Minister Stephen Harper, who had appointed Duffy as a senator *from PEI*, demanded that Duffy repay the expenses. Duffy refused. As the scandal grew, the prime minister's chief of staff Nigel Wright secretly gave Duffy the money so he could pay it back. (That's right, this scandal involves the Conservatives trying to *pay back* money.) When knowledge of Wright's payment became public, Wright resigned and the RCMP launched an investigation. Had Mike Duffy defrauded taxpayers and, in accepting Wright's offer, accepted a bribe as well? Charges were laid and a full-scale media frenzy began.

FALLOUT: The investigation of and subsequent trial over Duffy's $90,000 expense claims dragged on for two years and cost taxpayers $478,000. In the end, Mike Duffy was cleared of all charges. The damage had been done, though, and the ongoing trial almost certainly changed the course of the 2015 election.

GERALD BUTTS

MOVING COSTS FROM TORONTO TO OTTAWA: $126,669.56

Gerald Butts and Justin Trudeau are old school buddies, and when Justin became prime minister, Gerald became Justin's principle secretary and top adviser, the "BFF in the PMO," as the *Globe and Mail* described it. (The opening lines of the *Globe* profile read like a wedding invitation backstory: "Ever since Gerald Butts met Justin Trudeau in their days at McGill, the two men have shared a love of literature and a taste for adventure.")

In some circles, Gerald Butts is known as the "shadow prime minister." Others consider him Justin's "puppet-master." *Maclean's* describes him as "perhaps the most powerful unelected person in the nation's capital." This is the same Gerald Butts who denounced people who were laughing at Justin over his "peoplekind" comment as being in league with "alt-right nazis." (Gerald is very good at spotting nazis.)

When Butts moved from Toronto to Ottawa, he billed the government (i.e., taxpayers, i.e., you and me) more than $126,000 in relocation costs. That's right, Gerald Butts charged more in expenses *in one weekend* than Mike Duffy did in four years. (Okay, so we don't know how long it actually took him to "relocate." But it sure as hell wasn't four years. How one even goes about spending that sort of money to get from Toronto to Ottawa is an achievement in itself. I imagine each item being wrapped individually in silk and carried on velvet cushions by a procession of personal valets.)

FALLOUT: None. Number of police investigations: zero. Number of charges laid: nada. Number of media frenzies: zip. Instead, Butts simply assured us that his claims were perfectly legitimate and then agreed to pay back more than $40,000 of the money he took. Which is to say, we still had to foot $85,000 in moving fees for Justin's BFF. Gerald Butts did finally quit, but not because he suddenly had an attack of propriety regarding his expenses, heaven forbid, but due to the SNC-Lavalin scandal. Remember the old saying: A friend will pick you up at the airport, a good friend will help you move, but a best friend will resign under strange circumstances in order to provide a public distraction from your ham-handed dealings with a former justice minister. The old sayings are the best sayings.

"Fairness for middle class [*sic*] families. Hope and a future for middle class Canadians. That's our plan."

Because if there's anything middle-class families can relate to, it's $126,000 in moving costs for your BFF!

The unelected
Mike Duffy

The unelected
Gerald Butts

WHAT A LOUSY $150,000 WILL GET YOU IN THIS TOWN

The Conservative Party of Canada spent $600 on the cover of their final federal budget. Which still seems like a lot considering any kid with a printer and access to Photoshop could have whipped up something for free in five minutes. Six hundred bucks for a report cover, you say? Liberals: *Hold my beer.*

Are you ready for this? Are you sitting down? The Liberal Party of Canada spent more than $150,000 to design just the *cover* of their 2017 federal budget. Or, to put it in terms that Liberals would understand: *two* moving vans from Toronto to Ottawa. But that's okay, right? Because it's not like the government is running a huge deficit or anything? What, it is? Oh. But still, you can't put a price on something like this!

Actually, you can put a price on it: $157,000. (That's the official total. Other reports put it at a cool $212,230. So who knows?) Welcome to a New Era of Accountability™!

THIS COST US *AT LEAST* $157,000. MAYBE MORE.

At this point, you may have started to suspect that the Liberal Party of Canada has been throwing money around like a drunken sailor, but that's not fair—to drunks and sailors. After all, drunks and sailors generally throw around their own money, so they have to show at least *some* self-control. The Liberals are under no such restraints.

Paying advertising and marketing companies obscene amounts of money for basic services in return for government contracts. Reminds me of something, but I can't put my finger on it . . . What could it be? What could it be? What sort of precedent, what sort of déjà vu flashback to the last time the Liberals were in power could it be?

(See *sponsorship scandal*, Gomery Commission inquiry into Liberal corruption, etc., etc., etc.)

Every now and then, the media, through an oversight on their part, actually asks Justin a real question, rather than, say, obsessing over what kind of shampoo he uses or which socks he's wearing today. For example, Tom Clark of Global TV asked Justin, "Why are your deficits good and their deficits bad?"

"Well, deficits are a way of measuring the kind of growth and the kind of success that a government is actually able to create."

Justin Trudeau, overturning five hundred years of economic theory.

That's right! Deficits are now a measure of *success*. In the same way that an overdraft at the bank is a sign that things are going swell! So, the next time a collection agency contacts you about overdue accounts, just say, "No, no, no. You don't understand. That's just a sign of the type of success I'm having!"

Sorry I can't be with you—but how about Canada pledges $50M to @EduCannotWait to support education for women & girls around the world? Work for you? Let's do it.

*J*ustin Trudeau's infamous $50 million tweet, sent to impress an American TV host, seems to encapsulate everything about our PM that is so—I'm trying to think of a kind way of saying this—bloody annoying, so cringe-inducing.

Education for women and children, always a good cause. But of course, it really wasn't about the cause. It was about Justin. It's always about Justin. In this case, he was trying to buddy up to celebrity Trevor Noah, who was in South Africa hosting a global conference. Noah projected Justin's tweet onto the big screen, exclaiming, "This is amazing!" As though it were Justin's own money he was donating.

When Canadians responded that maybe, perhaps, instead of checking with Noah on whether $50 million "works for him," Justin might, oh, I don't know, check with us first, see if it "works" for Canadians.

It gets worse. As Justin's office huffed and puffed at the criticism, stopping just short of calling people nazis, they revealed that this wasn't a spontaneous gesture by a prime minister caught up in the moment. No. Justin's $50 million tweet had been planned *in advance*. Well in advance, in fact. As though that made it better! A major funding announcement . . . in a tweet.

Memo to the geniuses in the PMO: That doesn't make it better. It actually makes it worse. It means the entire thing was contrived, calculated, and staged. A stunt, in other words. Here's an idea: instead of selfies and cool tweets, maybe try, y'know, running the country for a while. Like grown-ups.

"One of the things that is important to me is fiscal responsibility."

Because saying something makes it true!

Justin & His Socks: A Tale for the Ages

SPEAKING OF TEEN IDOLS WITH NICE HAIR . . .

Pop singer Donny Osmond of "Puppy Love" fame was known for wearing purple socks. Is that wacky, or what? It was kind of his *thing.* Donny would flash his socks at teen fans and they would squeal in delight. He would answer questions about his socks in interviews. There are entire websites that revolve around Donny Osmond and his socks.

Justin clearly took note, but he went one better. Rather than simply *purple* socks, Justin would wear all kinds of colours and wacky designs—at important economic and political conferences, no less. While other leaders were discussing policies, our Justin became a media darling not because of his ideas, but because of his socks.

CANADA! **ON THE WORLD STAGE!**

When you suspect that your prime minister spends more time picking out his socks than he does on international and domestic affairs . . .

Donny Osmond explains his government's economic policies.

CANADA IN THE SPOTLIGHT: A ROUND-UP OF ACTUAL HEADLINES. SO ... YAY CANADA.

CANADA'S JUSTIN TRUDEAU IS WEARING CHEWBACCA SOCKS AND EVERYBODY'S FREAKING OUT
Daily Mirror

●

JUSTIN TRUDEAU'S ZANY 'STAR WARS' SOCK CHOICE IS THROWING THE INTERNET FOR A LOOP
Time

●

JUSTIN TRUDEAU'S 'STAR WARS' CHEWBACCA SOCKS CREATE SOCIAL MEDIA STIR
Hollywood Reporter

●

NO WORLD LEADER'S SOCKS HAVE EVER BEEN SO BELOVED
Huffington Post Canada

●

JUSTIN TRUDEAU'S SOCKS APPEAL
IS STARTING TO WEAR THIN

BY VINAY MENON

Toronto Star

●

You couldn't get away with this in any other line of work.

If your boss came to you and said, "Where's that earnings report?" and you responded by grinning and tugging up your pant legs to reveal socks with random numbers sewn into the pattern, you'd now be unemployed and possibly living under the care of a psychiatrist.

POP QUIZ: **KNOW YOUR SOCKS!**

Think it's easy coming up with the appropriate socks for the appropriate event? It's not. It's really, really hard. But this is just one of the many challenges Justin has had to overcome. Let's see if you can match up the right socks with the corresponding conference, remembering that in each case the media fixated on Justin's socks rather than ideas (or lack thereof).

1) Bloomberg Global Business Forum

2) Meeting with the prime minister of Ireland

3) Meeting with the former prime minister of Ireland

4) Economic forum in Switzerland

5) Pride church service in Toronto

6) Davos World Economic Forum

A) Chewbacca socks

B) Moose-print socks

C) R2-D2 and C-3PO socks

D) Jolly Rogers pirate socks

E) Yellow rubber ducky socks

F) Ramadan-themed rainbow socks

ANSWER KEY: 1-A, 2-B, 3-C, 4-D, 5-F, 6-E

GREAT MOMENTS IN CANADIAN POLITICAL ORATORY #3

Who Said It: John Diefenbaker or Justin Trudeau?

"I am a Canadian, free to speak without fear, free to worship in my own way, free to stand for what I think right, free to oppose what I believe wrong, free to choose those who shall govern my country."

or . . .

"I've also had the advantage of having to learn to put aside the people who think I'm great for the wrong reasons and developing a very strong sense of self, an awareness where you know what you are, what you're not, what you're good at, what you're not, is extremely important in a field that is so based around perceptions and connections with people."

"Ethics"

Maintaining the highest ethical standards is very important to Justin! And you know he's serious because he used a hashtag:

 Conservative ethics abuses have shaken Canadians' faith in Parliament. It's time to #raisethebar on accountability.

That was Justin in Opposition (for antonym, see *Justin in power*). If nothing else, Justin Trudeau has achieved two real milestones: he legalized weed and he was the first prime minister in history to be found guilty of violating Canada's Conflicts of Interest Act and he did it in style! Not just once, but four times! Makes you proud, don't it?

"I am committed to leading an open, honest government that is accountable to Canadians, lives up to the highest ethical standards, brings our country together, and applies the utmost care and prudence in the handling of public funds."

Apparently, he was just kidding.

FUN WITH TRUST FUNDS!

From a press scrum:

ROBERT FIFE, *GLOBE AND MAIL*: Prime Minister, you talk an awful lot about tax fairness. For fifteen years, the trust funds your father left you and your brother were allowed to grow in a sheltered vehicle . . . Why should you be able to take advantage of decades of tax planning rules that only the wealthiest Canadians can afford, a family trust, and deny business owners the same benefits?

JUSTIN TRUDEAU, PRIME MINISTER OF CANADA: Blah, blah, blah, middle class, blah, blah, blah, Stephen Harper, blah, blah, blah, Conservatives.

To which Fife complained, "You haven't answered the question."

Justin did, however, take a moment to stress that trust fund shelters such as the one that coddled him all those years are perfectly legal. He wanted to be very, very clear on that. *Remember kids, do as I say, not as I do!*

"I no longer have dealings with the way our family fortune is managed."

Justin Trudeau assuring middle-class voters that he is on their side, because nothing says "middle class" like the phrase "our family fortune"!

"A large percentage of small businesses are actually just ways for wealthier Canadians to save on taxes."

*J*ustin knows who the real villains are! Those devious small business owners. Farmers and doctors and the like. They're such greedy bastards.

To heck with lucrative offshore tax havens, it's those dastardly small business owners we need to worry about.

Remember kids: pipelines are bad, except when they're good; deficits are a sign of success; budgets will balance themselves; and it's the small business owners of this country who the government needs to be going after, not large corporations—and certainly not the offshore tax havens of the fabulously wealthy. It's Justin Economics in action!

"Low-income families don't benefit from tax breaks 'cause they don't pay taxes."

The prime minister of Canada explains how economics works to the House of Commons.

*U*m . . . That's not really it, Justin.

It's true there are refunds and rebates available, but I can assure you low-income families struggle with taxes, just like everyone else. Consumer taxes, in particular—sales taxes, carbon taxes, fuel surcharges, etc.—put a disproportionately *larger* burden on lower-income families than they do on the wealthy. You know, the type of people who can't afford offshore tax havens in the Cayman Islands. Then there was the transit tax credit for bus passes and the like, which did help lower-income students, the elderly, disabled people, etc. Justin cancelled that one.

ETHICS 101: BECAUSE WHO HASN'T FORGOTTEN ABOUT THEIR VILLA IN FRANCE AT SOME POINT?

Canada's finance minister Bill Morneau is splendidly rich. Practically a billionaire, in fact. How rich is he? When he was required to list his assets upon entering government, he forgot he had a private villa in France. (More specifically, he forgot to mention that he and his wife, Nancy—an heir to the McCain fortune—were joint owners of the private company that owned the villa.) An easy oversight, and one that most Canadians can relate to, I'm sure.

And let's be honest. If I owned a private villa in France, not only would I NOT forget it, I wouldn't let anyone else forget it either. *"Hello! Dave, is it? Nice to meet you, Dave. Say, did I ever mention that I OWN A FRICKIN' VILLA IN FRANCE?"*

Unfortunately, not disclosing his directorship in this company, or the full value of said villa in France, is a violation of Canada's ethics code. An investigation was launched, and justice was swift! The Conflict of Interest and Ethics Commissioner came down hard on Morneau. His punishment? A $200 fine.

Yup. Canada's multi-millionaire finance minister had to cough up two hundred bucks. So don't say the government doesn't take parliamentary ethics seriously! I've had parking tickets that cost me more than that. Morneau probably drops more than that on a shoe shine. Still, good to know that the Liberals are being held to the highest moral standard! Yay Canada!

Hang on to your hats, kids! You ain't seen nothing yet. That villa in France? That was just a warm-up. (See *private islands*, holidays on; *number of ethics rules broken*. Spoiler alert: four! So far.)

Wish You Were Here! Justin's Island Getaway

YOU THINK JUSTIN IS RICH? YOU THINK BILL MORNEAU IS LOADED?

They got nothing on Prince Shah Karim Al Hussaini, better known as Aga Khan IV. Spiritual leader of the world's Ismaili community, the Aga Khan has a personal net worth of $800 million, with business ventures that include horse breeding and a chain of luxury hotels. He also owns a private island in the Caribbean where the prime minister of Canada enjoyed a most excellent holiday. Because who among us hasn't taken a private helicopter to a billionaire's island while serving in public office? What's the big deal, right?

By the time it was all over, Justin would be found guilty of four separate violations of Canada's ethics laws. But I bet he got some amazing souvenir snapshots! Memories to last a lifetime! Talk about yer all-inclusives, eh?

"We don't see an issue on that."

Justin Trudeau, shrugging off objections to his private holiday on the Aga Khan's island. (Note the use of the Royal "We.")

*A*s well as being a jet-setting billionaire, Prince Karim is also the head of the Aga Khan Foundation, which lobbies the Canadian government for funds and receives tens of millions of dollars from Canada every year. The Aga Khan had recently been approved for a $15 million grant from the federal government for his Global Centre for Pluralism. So when Justin Trudeau decided to spend his holidays on the Aga Khan's private island in the Caribbean, it raised eyebrows, to say the least.

Justin flew down to the Bahamas with his family and friends, along with one of Trudeau's two full-time nannies, on a military jet, then took a private helicopter to the Aga Khan's island.

Canada's Conflict of Interest Act clearly states that ministers of the Crown are not allowed to "accept travel on non-commercial chartered or private aircraft for any purpose unless required in his or her capacity as a public office holder."

Justin didn't think the rules applied in this case because the Aga Khan was—and I quote—"an old friend." It came out later, however, that Justin had only ever been in the same room as the Aga Khan *once* in the last thirty years before he became leader of the Liberal Party of Canada. That's once in thirty years. So not exactly bosom buddies . . .

*I*t turns out the Christmas jaunt was not the first time Justin had availed himself of the Aga Khan's generosity. His family had vacationed on the same island six months earlier.

It gets better: Just two days *before* Justin's family's first trip to the island, a representative of the Aga Khan requested an official meeting with the prime minister to discuss, among other items, the $15 million grant from the federal government mentioned earlier. The meeting was approved and went ahead a few weeks later.

At this point, if alarm bells aren't ringing, you aren't paying attention.

Anyone with an ethical compass could have seen the conflict. And yet, there he was, our glorious prime minister, happily accepting a luxury holiday, free of charge, at an exclusive private island owned by a billionaire whose foundation was lobbying the very government Justin represents. The fact that Justin saw nothing wrong with this is remarkable, amazing, unbelievable even.

Justin would later brush aside what he called these "supposed ethical issues" raised by the Opposition as nothing more than a "personal attack." But just *two days* after blustering that "we don't see an issue" with the trip, Justin was found guilty of having breached the Conflict of Interest Act on four separate charges, becoming the first prime minister to have done so.

Life comes at you fast.

*T*he Aga Khan may have provided Justin, his family, and some of Justin's close friends with a free holiday, but the trip itself wasn't exactly free. The added cost of Justin's jaunt to the Bahamas, in terms of extra RCMP security, Department of National Defence jets, Global Affairs Canada costs, and other expenses: $215,398.

And even then, the initial cost, as tabled in Parliament, was $127,187. It took an Access-to-Information request to reveal that the actual amount was 70 per cent higher than claimed. No wonder the Liberals aren't fans of Access to Information.

Fun side fact: Justin's use of a military jet for his family vacation to the Aga Khan's island emitted as much CO_2 as the average Canadian does in a year! Yay Justin!

*O*ur old friend Nathan Cullen was curious about how much a comparable all-expenses paid vacation for nine people to an exclusive private island would have cost. (That was how many guests travelled to the Aga Khan's island: Justin, his family, a full-time nanny, and others, including Anna Gainey, president of the Liberal Party of Canada.) He contacted several travel agencies and calculated that a similar vacation would have cost $100,000.

This raised a more serious question. As Mr. Cullen put it: "I also want to know the difference between asking for a $100,000 vacation and asking for $100,000 in an envelope."

Mr. Prime Minister, we're still waiting on your answer!

GUILTY, GUILTY, GUILTY, GUILTY

On December 20, 2017—just *two days* after Justin Trudeau assured Canadians that there were no issues with his trip—Canada's ethics commissioner ruled that the prime minister had violated four separate provisions of the Conflict of Interest Act, specifically, sections 5, 11, 12, and 21.

Section 5 requires that a public office holder arrange his or her private affairs in a manner that will prevent the public office holder from being in a conflict of interest.

THE COMMISSIONER RULED:

> Mr. Trudeau failed to meet the general duty set out in section 5 when he and his family vacationed on the Aga Khan's private island.

Section 11 prohibits a public office holder or a member of his or her family from accepting any gift or other advantage that might reasonably be seen to have been given to influence the public office holder. Free vacations would certainly fall under this definition of a gift.

THE COMMISSIONER RULED:

> I found that these gifts could reasonably be seen to have been given to influence Mr. Trudeau in the exercise of an official power, duty or function.

Section 12 prohibits ministers and members of their families from accepting travel on private aircraft unless it is required as part of the minister's official duties.

THE COMMISSIONER RULED:

Mr. Trudeau contravened section 12 when he and his family accepted travel provided by the Aga Khan on private aircraft. The travel was not required as part of his official duties.

Section 21 requires that public office holders recuse themselves from any discussion, decision, debate, or vote on any matter in respect of which they would be in a conflict of interest.

THE COMMISSIONER RULED:

I found that Mr. Trudeau contravened section 21 when he failed to recuse himself from two discussions during which he had an opportunity to improperly further the private interests of the [Aga Khan's] Global Centre for Pluralism.

As the ethics commissioner noted, this violation happened shortly before Mr. Trudeau's family vacationed on the Aga Khan's private island.

THE COMMISSIONER CONCLUDED:

Mr. Trudeau failed to arrange his private affairs in a manner that would prevent him from being placed in a conflict of interest. Neither Mr. Trudeau nor his family should have vacationed on the Aga Khan's private island.

UM, ER, UM, AH . . .

If nothing else, with the Aga Khan affair, Justin Trudeau made history. He became the first sitting prime minister to be found guilty of ethics violations under the Conflict of Interest Act. (This was also the first time that both a prime minister *and* a finance minister had been found in breach of Canada's ethics laws. See *Bill Morneau*, private villa in France.)

The consequences? Not a goddamn thing. Was Justin impeached? Nope. In Canada we don't impeach our leaders. We can't. Was he fined? Forced to step down? At the very least, did he have to pay for all those freebies he accepted? Nope.

The worst Justin had to face were some awkward questions at a parliamentary news scrum. That was the sum total of the consequences.

THE PRESS FINALLY ASKS A HARD QUESTION:

"How could that not have occurred to you? With all due respect, you were going to take a free holiday from someone you consider a friend—but obviously you have a different definition of a friend than the commissioner. You knew that they had a lobbying registry, that they were set up to lobby the government. How could it not have occurred to you that that might not have been okay?"

Justin's reply? Direct. Precise. No-nonsense.

"The fact is we work, ahh . . . [long pause] Sorry, let me just try to reorder—reorder the thoughts. We, um, worked with, ah, the, ah, lobby, conflict of interest commissioner, ahh, on a regular basis, on a broad range of issues when the issues come up. On this issue of a family vacation with a personal friend, um, it wasn't considered that there would be an issue there. Obviously—obviously there was a mistake."

The unimpeachable Justin Trudeau, ladies and gentlemen!

JUST PLAYIN' CATCH AND SKIPPIN' STONES.

It got worse (or better, from a purely entertainment point of view). Here is Justin trying desperately to spin the scandal in terms that will resonate with those mythical middle-class voters he's so enamoured with:

......

"Aga Khan is someone who has been a long-time friend of my family's, a friend of mine, a friend, ah, to Canada as well, ah, and for me to look for a place to have a quiet vacation where I could have quality family time is, ah, something we all look for with our families."

So you see? It was all about *quality time* with the kids. And that's something we can all relate to, right? Because who among us hasn't jetted off to a billionaire's private island for free? Right?

FROM AN EARLIER Q & A WITH JUSTIN TRUDEAU:

"What's your greatest extravagance?"

"Travel. Once a year, I make sure to take Sophie and the kids away to some amazing place."

NOTE: He doesn't say he actually *pays* for those trips himself.

"I think people are starting to see that I'm actually reasonably fit for this office."

Justin Trudeau, in spite of everything!

In fairness, he said this *before* the runaway deficits, failed electoral reform, Bollywood dance moves, $50 million tweet, and being found guilty of violating Canada's conflict of interest laws on four counts. But how could he have known?

Your Prime Minister in Action!

NEW ERA!

For those keeping track:

The number of times the Evil Stephen Harper™ was called before the ethics commissioner during the course of his nine and a half years in office: zero.

The number of times Justin Trudeau was called before the ethics commissioner in his first two years alone: two? three? maybe four? . . . approximately. No one knows for sure because *he won't say*. And all of it over an innocent trip to a billionaire's private island. Poor Justin, everyone is so mean to him.

Which brings us to the most depressing section in this entire book. You may want to pour yourself a Scotch before we go on.

*J*ustin promised a new era "of openness and transparency!" He also said that he would appear in the House to face any questions the Opposition had. Note: He didn't say he would *answer* the questions. Just that he would be there.

The Opposition had a simple query:

HOW MANY TIMES DID THE PRIME MINISTER MEET WITH THE ETHICS COMMISSIONER?

That's it. All he had to say was a number. They asked him this question *eighteen times in a row*, and he didn't answer it, not once. He just repeated the same talking points—again and again and again and again and again. *Eighteen times!* It really was quite remarkable, even by Justin Trudeau standards.

Shall we begin our descent into the rabbit hole?

*T*he following is a transcript from question period in the House for May 10, 2017, where Prime Minister Justin Trudeau avoided answering a simple question eighteen times in a row.

And these are just the *highlights*; for a complete rundown of the entire session, including interruptions, Speaker admonishments, and rambling digressions by Justin about "democracy" and "the middle class"—none of which, of course, has anything to do with the question at hand: How many times have you met with the ethics commissioner?—you can read it in its entirety online at: *Parliament of Canada, House of Commons Official Record (Hansard).*

If you're thinking, *Not answering a question eighteen times doesn't seem so bad*, I recommend you read what follows from beginning to end without skimming and tell me you don't feel like you need a shower afterward.

If nothing else, it makes for a fun parlour game! Invite eighteen of your closest friends over to play the parts of the various MPs. (For the role of Justin, a tape recorder will suffice, as he gives the same non-answer every single time.) Either way, you really do have to read it aloud to get the full impact.

QUESTION PERIOD, HOUSE OF COMMONS, MAY 10, 2017

Mr. Jacques Gourde (CPC): How many times has the Prime Minister met with the Conflict of Interest and Ethics Commissioner to discuss his loose ethics?

Right Hon. Justin Trudeau (LIB): Mr. Speaker, as you know, I am always pleased to work with the Conflict of Interest and Ethics Commissioner to answer any questions she may have.

Mr. Jacques Gourde (CPC): Mr. Speaker, it is a very simple question, but mainly it is a question of trust.

What Canadians are hearing is that there are laws that apply to them but that do not apply to the Prime Minister.

I will repeat my question. How many times has the Prime Minister met with the Conflict of Interest and Ethics Commissioner?

Right Hon. Justin Trudeau (LIB): Mr. Speaker, as I have always said, I am very pleased to meet with the Conflict of Interest and Ethics Commissioner and work with her to answer any questions she may have on this subject or any other.

....

Hon. Candice Bergen (CPC): The question is not if he is happy or satisfied or feeling good about meeting the Ethics Commissioner. Has the Prime Minister met with the Ethics Commissioner, and if so, how many times? It is very, very simple.

Right Hon. Justin Trudeau (LIB): Mr. Speaker, I am pleased to work with the Conflict of Interest and Ethics Commissioner to answer any questions she may have. That is what Canadians expect of the Prime Minister and that is exactly what I am doing.

Hon. Candice Bergen (CPC): Mr. Speaker, what Canadians expect is that their Prime Minister would give a clear answer to a clear and a simple question. If he has something to hide, then Canadians want to know that as well. I would suggest, if he wants to send Canadians the message that he has nothing to hide, that he answer the question.

How many times has the Prime Minister met with the Ethics Commissioner?

Right Hon. Justin Trudeau (LIB): Mr. Speaker, I am very happy to work with and answer the Conflict of Interest and Ethics Commissioner's questions . . . Canadians expect the Prime Minister to work with the Conflict of Interest and Ethics Commissioner any time she has questions, and that is exactly what I have been doing.

....

Mr. John Brassard (CPC): Mr. Speaker, the Prime Minister keeps saying he is happy to meet with the Ethics Commissioner and answer any questions she might have, but he is really playing a game of political survivor by outwitting, outplaying, and outlasting the Ethics Commissioner over his vacation to billionaire island.

It has been asked four times already. I do not even know why I am trying, to be frank, but I will repeat the simple question. How many times has the Prime Minister met with the Ethics Commissioner?

Right Hon. Justin Trudeau (LIB): Mr. Speaker, I am happy, as should be any member of this House, to work with the Ethics Commissioner and answer any questions that she may have. I think that is important.

Mr. John Brassard (CPC): What a charade, Mr. Speaker . . .

He has been asked five times today about the Ethics Commissioner. For the sake of my colleagues, I will ask it again. How many times, how many times, how many times, how many times, how many times, and how many times has he met with the Ethics Commissioner?

Right Hon. Justin Trudeau (LIB): I will work with and answer the questions that the Conflict of Interest and Ethics Commissioner may have.

....

Hon. Thomas Mulcair (NDP): Mr. Speaker, if the Prime Minister truly believes in the importance of question period, if he sincerely believes in transparency and accountability, he is going to have to find it somewhere inside himself to answer this very basic question, because it only concerns him and he knows the answer.

He is being investigated by the Ethics Commissioner. How many times has the Prime Minister communicated with the Ethics Commissioner? Answer the question.

Right Hon. Justin Trudeau (LIB): Mr. Speaker, when asked the same question, I will give the same answer. I am happy to work with the Ethics Commissioner on any questions she may have.

Mr. Alexander Nuttall (CPC): For the eighth time, how many times have you met with the Ethics Commissioner?

Right Hon. Justin Trudeau (LIB): Mr. Speaker, I am happy to sit and work with the Ethics Commissioner on answering any of the questions she may have.

....

Mr. Gérard Deltell (CPC): I would like to ask him a very clear question for the ninth time. How many times did he meet with the Conflict of Interest and Ethics Commissioner? I would like a clear answer. Canadians want to know.

Right Hon. Justin Trudeau (LIB): Mr. Speaker, I am very happy to work with the Conflict of Interest and Ethics Commissioner to answer any questions she may have.

Mr. Alain Rayes (CPC): This should be an easy answer: one, two, or three times. I am sure it is less than five times.

This is a simple question. Was it one time, or was it zero?

Right Hon. Justin Trudeau (LIB): Mr. Speaker, I am very happy to work with the Conflict of Interest and Ethics Commissioner to answer any questions she may have.

....

Hon. Pierre Poilievre (CPC): How many times did the Prime Minister meet with the Ethics Commissioner with regard to the investigation into his trip to billionaire island?

Right Hon. Justin Trudeau (LIB): Mr. Speaker, I am happy to answer as many questions as the members opposite have, but if they ask the same question, they will keep getting the same answer. I am pleased to work with the Conflict of Interest and Ethics Commissioner to answer any questions that she might have.

Mrs. Cathy McLeod (CPC): I will try a different angle. Was it zero times the Prime Minister met with the Ethics Commissioner, was it one to five, or was it six to ten?

Right Hon. Justin Trudeau (LIB): Mr. Speaker, I am happy to work with the Ethics Commissioner on any questions that she might have.

....

Mr. David Sweet (CPC): Could you please tell the House how many times you have met with the Ethics Commissioner?

Right Hon. Justin Trudeau (LIB): Mr. Speaker, I am happy to work with the Ethics Commissioner to answer any questions she may have.

Mr. David Anderson (CPC): Mr. Speaker, the Prime Minister broke the law. He accepted gifts worth thousands of dollars on billionaire island. He is under investigation by the Ethics Commissioner. His obligation is to be honest with Canadians. What is he covering up here? How many times has he communicated with the Ethics Commissioner?

Right Hon. Justin Trudeau (LIB): Mr. Speaker, I am pleased to work with the Ethics Commissioner to answer any questions that she might have.

....

Hon. Peter Kent (CPC): Mr. Speaker . . . Just how many times has he met the Ethics Commissioner?

Right Hon. Justin Trudeau (LIB): Mr. Speaker, I am happy to work with the Ethics Commissioner to answer any questions she might have.

Hon. Michelle Rempel (CPC): Mr. Speaker, a well-known French writer once said, "Man is not what he thinks he is, he is what he hides." Will the Prime Minister stop hiding the truth, show Canadians what he is actually made of, and tell Canadians how many times he has met with the Ethics Commissioner?

Right Hon. Justin Trudeau (LIB): Mr. Speaker, I am happy to work with the Ethics Commissioner to answer any questions she may have.

Mrs. Kelly Block (CPC): How many times has the Prime Minister met with the Ethics Commissioner?

Right Hon. Justin Trudeau (LIB): Mr. Speaker, I am pleased to work with the Ethics Commissioner and to answer any questions that she may have.

Mr. Luc Berthold (CPC): Why does the Prime Minister refuse to answer Canadians?
    How many times did he meet with the Conflict of Interest and Ethics Commissioner?

Right Hon. Justin Trudeau (LIB): Mr. Speaker, I am very happy to work with the Conflict of Interest and Ethics Commissioner to answer any questions she may have.

Stop the Presses!

I really thought that Justin had topped himself with four—count 'em *four*—ethics violations over his visit to a billionaire's private island. (Justin Trudeau, Champion of the Middle Class!) But in 2019, it was announced that Justin was now under his *fifth* ethics investigation, in this case over allegations of political interference into a criminal prosecution.

When Justin named the highly respected First Nations lawyer and former Crown Prosecutor Jody Wilson-Raybould to the post of Justice Minister and Attorney General, it was heralded as an important milestone for Indigenous women. Alas, Justin would soon receive a lesson in integrity from Ms. Wilson-Raybould.

She became concerned that Justin and his staff were trying to politically interfere in the criminal prosecution of a Liberal-friendly Quebec firm, SNC-Lavalin, which had been charged with bribery and corruption in the case of Libyan dictator Muammer Gaddafi's son who had reportedly been paid millions and plied with Montreal prostitutes by SNC-Lavalin during his visit to Canada. (SNC-Lavalin had also illegally donated more than $100K to the Liberals, which the Liberals were forced to return, hence the use of my phrase "Liberal-friendly firm.")

After Wilson-Raybould refused to cut a deal with the company, in spite of ongoing pressure from Justin Trudeau and the PMO, she was unceremoniously dumped as Justice Minister, which the Liberals insisted was just a coincidence. Possible political interference in an ongoing criminal prosecution? Those are serious, serious charges. And yet, a Liberal majority justice committee quickly shut down the inquiry saying, essentially, "Move along folks! Nothing to see here!"

JUSTIN'S **WHEEL O' EXCUSES!**

Why did Justin Trudeau remove Jody Wilson-Raybould as Justice Minister? Surely it had nothing to do with the fact that she wouldn't cave in and cut SNC-Lavalin a deal at the prime minister's behest. The excuses came fast and furious, ladies and gentlemen! To find out what the reason is this week, simply, spin the wheel!

*"Gardens need a lot of care. But if you love your garden,
you don't mind working in it, and waiting.
Then in the proper season you will surely see it flourish."*

Chance the Gardener in Jerzy Kosiński's *Being There*

Acknowledgements

First and foremost, a huge thank you to the indomitable Sophia Muthuraj at Simon & Schuster for her unflagging enthusiasm, keen sense of humour, input, and tireless efforts on behalf of this project. You did a terrific job! Kevin Hanson, Publisher and President of Simon & Schuster Canada, supported this book from the start, which was crucial and much appreciated. Interior design director Paul Dippolito, cover designer Paul Barker, copyeditor Melody Frank, and publicist Jessica Rattray: thank you all for the wonderful work you did on this!

Sources

INTRODUCTION

3   "Canada's Stock Market Is": David Thomas, "Canada's Stock Market Is the Worst in the World Right Now," *MoneySense*, February 20, 2018, https://www.moneysense.ca/save/investing/stocks/canadas-stock-market-is-the-worst-in-the-world-right-now/.

3   "The Canadian Dollar Is": Rajeshni Naidu-Ghelani, "Loonie Falls After Poloz Suggests He's Not Ready to Take Away 'Punch Bowl,'" CBC News, March 13, 2018, https://www.cbc.ca/news/business/stephen-poloz-canadian-dollar-loonie-1.4574167.

3   "Justin Trudeau's Budget": "Justin Trudeau's Budget Still Hasn't Balanced Itself," *London Free Press*, March 1, 2018, https://lfpress.com/opinion/editorials/editorial-justin-trudeaus-budget-still-hasnt-balanced-itself.

3   "Science-Loving Government": "Science-Loving Government Cuts Funding for Science," *Globe and Mail*, January 23, 2018, https://www.theglobeandmail.com/opinion/editorials/globe-editorial-science-loving-government-cuts-funding-for-science/article37711890/.

3   "Trudeau's Perpetual Deficits": Tom Brodbeck, "Trudeau's Perpetual Deficits Will Cause Lasting Harm," *Winnipeg Sun*, February 27, 2018, https://winnipegsun.com/news/provincial/trudeaus-perpetual-deficits-will-cause-lasting-harm.

FRAT BOY

7   "The intensity, the excitement": Jeff Green, "Sex, Pizza, and Politics with Justin Trudeau," *Hamilton Spectator*, October 13, 2011, https://www.thespec.com/news-story/2219070-sex-pizza-and-politics-with-justin-trudeau/.

8   "I don't read the newspapers": Jonathon Gatehouse, "'When I Run': Justin Trudeau Considers Politics," *Maclean's*, December 23, 2002, https://www.macleans.ca/politics/ottawa/when-i-run-justin-trudeau-considers-politics-from-the-archives/.

9   "People in the street": Guy Lawson, "Trudeau's Canada, Again," *New York Times Magazine*, December 8, 2015, https://www.nytimes.com/2015/12/13/magazine/trudeaus-canada-again.html.

10   "It's very, very cool": Ibid

12   "I'm not going to go": "Justin Trudeau's Mysterious Connection with Canadians," Global News, April 7, 2013, https://globalnews.ca/news/461252/justin-trudeaus-mysterious-connection-with-canadians/.

13   "I'm going to defer": Brian Lilley, "Pole Position: Our PM-in-Waiting Defers, Again, to Experts on Arctic Seabed Issue," *Toronto Sun*, December 5, 2013, https://torontosun.com/2013/12/05/pole-position-our-pm-in-waiting-defers-again-to-experts-on-arctic-seabed-issue/wcm/52322832-f7e7-49c1-b781-f320381d9642.

14   "They will come at me": Justin Trudeau, "Justin Trudeau Takes a Gamble on Staying Positive," interviewed by Peter Mansbridge, CBC News, April 17, 2013, https://www.cbc.ca/news/canada/justin-trudeau-takes-a-gamble-on-staying-positive-1.1357601.

16   "What happens if": Maura Forrest, "Five Things We Learned About Science (and Other Stuff) from Justin Trudeau and Bill Nye," *National Post*, March 6, 2018, https://nationalpost.com/news/politics/five-things-we-learned-about-science-and-other-stuff-from-justin-trudeau-and-bill-nye.

17   "Twerp": Evan Solomon, "Why David Suzuki Called Justin Trudeau a Twerp," *Maclean's*, September 26, 2015, https://www.macleans.ca/politics/ottawa/why-david-suzuki-called-justin-trudeau-a-twerp/.

17   "You're for the development": Ibid.

18   "At one point people": Justin Trudeau, "Justin Trudeau: Man Who Would Be PM Discusses His Past, His Politics," interviewed by Lisa LaFlamme, *W5*, CTV News, October 18, 2014, https://www.ctvnews.ca/w5/justin-trudeau-man-who-would-be-pm-discusses-his-past-his-politics-1.2059548.

JUSTIN: BEYOND SPACE & TIME

21   "We have to rethink": Monte Solberg, "Justin Is Beyond Infinity," *Brantford Expositor*, September 21, 2014, http://www.brantfordexpositor.ca/2014/09/21/justin-is-beyond-infinity.

22   "The way forward": James Fitz-Morris and Catherine Tunney, "Justin Trudeau Promises 'Canadian Approach' to Climate Change," CBC News, November 23, 2015, http://www.cbc.ca/news/politics/trudeau-first-ministers-meet-climate-change-1.3331290.

23   "The world is moving": "Justin Trudeau Speaks at 2018 Deloitte Canada Partner Meeting," Deloitte Canada Conference, September 7, 2018, video, 42:30, http://www.cpac.ca/en/programs/headline-politics/episodes/64380451.

23   "Entropy": "Entropy," Merriam Webster, https://www.merriam-webster.com/dictionary/entropy.

24   "There is no core identity": Guy Lawson, "Trudeau's Canada, Again" *New York Times Magazine*, December 8, 2015, https://www.nytimes.com/2015/12/13/magazine/trudeaus-canada-again.html.

25   "The nation is no longer": Ibid

26   "Responsibilizing": "Justin Trudeau Speaks at 2018 Deloitte Canada Partner Meeting," Deloitte Canada Conference.

28   "You cannot let yourself": "Prime Minister Justin Trudeau," *60 Minutes*, CBS News, March 6, 2016, https://www.cbsnews.com/news/60-minutes-prime-minister-trudeau/.

29   "I'm much more focused": "Interview with Justin Trudeau," *The West Block*, Global News, September 26, 2015, available at: https://www.youtube.com/watch?v=py1t3tGqCuk.

JUSTIN TRUDEAU: INTERNATIONAL MAN OF MYSTERY!

33   "I won the birth lottery": Joseph Brean, "Justin Trudeau on the Burden of Greatness," *National Post*, November 8, 2006, https://www.pressreader.com/canada/national-post-latest-edition/20061108/281517926620316.

34   "We grew up in": Karl Moore, "One-on-One Interview with Justin Trudeau," *Forbes*, November 4, 2015, https://www.forbes.com/sites/karlmoore/2015/11/04/an-one-on-one-with-canadas-new-prime-minister-justin-trudeau/#b534995ea062.

35   "One of the big difficulties": "Exclusive Interview with Justin Trudeau (Uncut)," *Salam Toronto*, March 27, 2014, YouTube video, 33:32, https://www.youtube.com/watch?v=W8NOqhCg_eQ.

36   "My maternal grandfather": David Aktin, "Say That Again? Unintended Zingers from Trudeau's National Listening Tour," *National Post*, January 17, 2017, https://nationalpost

.com/news/politics/say-that-again-unintended -zingers-from-trudeaus-national-listening-tour.

37   Justin has also suggested: Justin Lang, "Trudeau's Backpacking Guide to International Relations," *National Post*, April 10, 2014, https:// nationalpost.com/opinion/justin-ling-trudeaus -backpacking-guide-to-international-relations.

37   "If I'm sitting here": "Justin Trudeau on Syria, Republicanism, and Being a Sex Symbol," *Newsnight*, BBC, YouTube video, 7:12, November 25, 2015, https://www.youtube.com/ watch?v=wcRbLBa9B_8.

38   "Humility is very important": Martin Patriquin, "Does Justin Trudeau Risk Being Overexposed?" *Maclean's*, August 26, 2016, https://www.macleans.ca/politics/does-justin -trudeau-risk-being-overexposed/.

39   "There's an awful lot": Ibid.

40   "My stepfather was born": Taint Koch, Christian Stenzel, and Daniel Biskup, "Is It Annoying to Be the Anti-Trump?" *BILD*, July 9, 2017, https://www.bild.de/politik/ausland/ bild-international/interview-justin-trudeau -canada-is-it-annoying-to-be-the-anti-trump -52463994.bild.html.

SENSEI

42   And given that: Jeff Wallenfeldt, "Justin Trudeau," Britannica, March 7, 2019, accessed https://www.britannica.com/biography/ Justin-Trudeau.

42   Most of that: Althia Raj, The Contender: The Justin Trudeau Story, *Huffington Post Canada*, March 3, 2013, http://big.assets.huffingtonpost .com/ContenderV2.pdf.

42   "During an interview": Jeff Lee, "Justin Trudeau: The B.C. Connection That Helped Make a Prime Minister," *Vancouver Sun*, October 24, 2015, http://www.vancouversun.com/news/ justin+trudeau+connection+that+helped +make+prime+minister/11463772/story.html.

43   "There is nothing he": Robert Matas,

"I'm Passionate About Politics Because I'm Passionate About Life," *Globe and Mail*, February 3, 2001, https://www .theglobeandmail.com/news/national/ im-passionate-about-politics-because -impassionate-about-life/article1030012/.

44   "I'm a teacher": Canadian Press, "Trudeau Wins Montreal Riding Nomination," CBC News, April 29, 2007, https://www.cbc.ca/ news/canada/trudeau-wins-montreal-riding -nomination-1.657245.

45   Current tuition at West Point: "Fees & Scholarships," West Point Grey Academy, https://www.wpga.ca/admission/fees— scholarships (accessed March 4, 2019).

MEET YER CANDIDATE!

48   Justin *tried* to: Jeff Wallenfeldt, "Justin Trudeau," Britannica, March 7, 2019, accessed https://www.britannica.com/biography/ Justin-Trudeau.

51   "Let us be English": John A. Macdonald, during confederation talks of 1864.

51   "I had to learn": Justin Trudeau, "Justin Trudeau: Man Who Would Be PM Discusses His Past, His Politics," interview by Lisa LaFlamme, *W5*, CTV News, October 18, 2014, video, 6:27, https://www.ctvnews.ca/w5/justin -trudeau-man-who-would-be-pm-discusses-his -past-his-politics-1.2059548.

NATIONAL SECURITY STUFF

55   "Investigative national security": "Prime Minister Justin Trudeau," *Live with Kelly and Ryan*, ABC, June 5, 2017, available at: https:// www.youtube.com/watch?v=p5R1lMOhwpc.

56   Public safety minister Ralph Goodale: Lee Berthiaume, "Baloney Meter: Are Liberals Welcoming ISIL Returnees to Canada with Open Arms?" CBC News, November 30, 2017, https://www.cbc.ca/ news/politics/isil-returnees-baloney-meter -1.4426096.

56 At the town hall: "Trudeau Compares Returning ISIS Fighters to Greek & Italian Immigrants," Cdn Infidels, YouTube video, 2:23, February 4, 2018, https://www.youtube.com/watch?v=OwHwD58R9cg.

57 "Well, I can tell": Joe O'Connor, "Justin Trudeau vs Justin Trudeau: A Brief History of a Prime Minister and His (Epic) Gaffes," *National Post*, February 6, 2018, https://nationalpost.com/news/politics/justin-trudeau-vs-justin-trudeau-a-brief-history-of-a-prime-minister-and-his-epic-gaffes.

58 "If you don't want": *Power & Politics*, CBC, June 23, 2015.https://www.cbc.ca/player/play/2670343050.

60 "There is no question": Justin Trudeau, "Justin Trudeau Takes a Gamble on Staying Positive," interview by Peter Mansbridge, CBC News, April 17, 2013, video, 14:15, https://www.cbc.ca/news/canada/justin-trudeau-takes-a-gamble-on-staying-positive-1.1357601.

62 "There's a lot of people": Josh Skurnik, "Trudeau: Drop Parkas, Not Bombs," *Toronto Sun*, November 7, 2014, https://torontosun.com/2014/11/07/trudeau-drop-parkas-not-bombs/wcm/bc38d56c-08f3-4cf0-a718-2ad1c8739894.

62 "Never mind airstrikes": Ibid.

WHIRLED AFFAIRS

64 The ambassador from: Lee-Ann Goodman, "Trudeau's Hockey-Ukraine Joke Ripped by Conservatives," *Huffington Post Canada*, February 24, 2014, https://www.huffingtonpost.ca/2014/02/24/trudeau-hockey-ukraine-tories-ndp_n_4847789.html?utm_hp_ref=canada-politics.

64 He would later: Leslie MacKinnon, "Justin Trudeau Apologizes for Ukraine Joke," *CBC News*, February 25, 2014, https://www.cbc.ca/news/politics/justin-trudeau-apologizes-for-ukraine-joke-1.2550790.

65 "It's very worrisome": *Tout le monde en parle*, Radio-Canada, February 23, 2014, http://ici.radio-canada.ca/emissions/tout_le_monde_en_parle/saison10/document.asp?idDoc=329431.

66 "There's a level of": Jen Gerson, "At Toronto Fundraiser, Justin Trudeau Seemingly Admires China's 'Basic Dictatorship,'" *National Post*, November 8, 2013, https://nationalpost.com/news/politics/justin-trudeau-seemingly-admires-chinas-basic-dictatorship-at-toronto-fundraiser.

67 So how about: Ibid.

67 Then there's this: Martin Empson, "Focus on China: The East Is Green?" *Socialist Review* 432 (February 25, 2018): http://socialistreview.org.uk/432/focus-china-east-green.

68 "let out his": Jen Gerson, "At Toronto fundraiser, Justin Trudeau Seemingly Admires China's 'basic dictatorship'."

68 "It seems to be": "Justin Trudeau's 'Foolish' China Remarks Spark Anger," CBC News, November 9, 2013, https://www.cbc.ca/news/canada/toronto/justin-trudeau-s-foolish-china-remarks-spark-anger-1.2421351.

NAMASTE, YO!

71 "silly, diminished and desperate": Barkha Dutt, "Trudeau's India Trip Is a Total Disaster—and He Has Only Himself to Blame," *Washington Post*, February 22, 2018, https://www.washingtonpost.com/news/global-opinions/wp/2018/02/22/trudeaus-india-trip-is-a-total-disaster-and-he-has-himself-to-blame/?utm_term=.5f4300f4fd91.

72 "Our countries both marked": Tarek Fatah, "All Trudeau Needed to Do Was Denounce the Khalistan Movement," *Toronto Sun*, February 24, 2018, https://torontosun.com/opinion/columnists/fatah-all-trudeau-needed-to-do-was-denounce-the-khalistan-movement.

73 "Canadian Prime Minister Justin": Indrani Bagchi, "Why Trudeau's Disaster Trip May

Trigger a Reset in India-Canada Ties," *Times of India*, February 25, 2018, http://timesofindia.indiatimes.com/articleshow/63058415.cms?utm_source=contentofinterest&utm_medium=text&utm_campaign=cppst.

73 "India Trip Raises Eyebrows": Anirudh Bhattacharyya, "Justin Trudeau's 'Unusual' India Trip Raises Eyebrows, Panned by Canada Watchdog," *Hindustan Times*, February 20, 2018, https://www.hindustantimes.com/world-news/trudeau-s-unusual-india-visit-raises-eyebrows-criticised-by-canada-watchdog/story-Xg6UmLGX4g3AkPHhD87oVL.html.

73 "Too Flashy Even for an Indian?": "Trudeau Family's Attire Too Flashy Even for an Indian?" *Outlook*, February 21, 2018, https://www.outlookindia.com/website/story/trudeau-familys-attire-too-indian-even-for-an-indian/308603.

73 "Justin Trudeau's Bhangra": Sherya Das, "Justin Trudeau's Bhangra in Delhi Leaves Many Unhappy, Here's Why," *Indian Express*, February 23, 2018, https://indianexpress.com/article/trending/viral-videos-trending/justin-trudeau-bhangra-in-delhi-twitter-reactions-5075060/.

73 "Trudeau Shoots Himself": "Trudeau Shoots Himself in the Foot Once Again," *New Indian Express*, March 1, 2018, http://www.newindianexpress.com/nation/2018/mar/01/trudeau-shoots-himself-in-the-foot-once-again-1780440.html.

76 "Over a billion dollars": Kelly McParland, "Welcome Home, Prime Minister! How Was the Trip? Oh. I See," *National Post*, February 26, 2018, https://nationalpost.com/opinion/kelly-mcparland-welcome-home-prime-minister-how-was-the-trip-oh-i-see.

77 After an eight-day: Canadian Press, "Trudeau's Contested Trip to India Cost Upwards of $1.5 Million, Documents Show," Global News, June 20, 2018, https://globalnews.ca/news/4287371/trudeaus-india-trip-1-5-million/.

PROMISES, PROMISES

80 "What Trudeau proved himself": Aaron Wherry, "Trudeau's Promise of Electoral Reform: From 'We Can Do Better' to Accusations of Betrayal," CBC News, February 5, 2017, https://www.cbc.ca/news/politics/wherry-trudeau-electoral-reform-promise-betrayal-1.3962386.

81 "2015 will be the last": "Electoral Reform," 2015 Liberal Party Platform, https://www.liberal.ca/realchange/electoral-reform/; "Canada Throne Speech 2015 full text: A Complete Copy of Trudeau's First Agenda," *National Post*, December 4, 2015, https://nationalpost.com/news/politics/canada-throne-speech-2015-full-text.

82 "Canadians elect governments": Alex Boutilier and Alex Ballingall, "Trudeau Insists Election Reform Still on Table," *Toronto Star*, December 2, 2016, https://www.thestar.com/news/canada/2016/12/02/trudeau-insists-election-reform-still-on-table.html.

83 "Trudeau Insists Election Reform": Ibid.

83 "Trudeau Abandons Pledge": Alex Boutilier, "Trudeau Abandons Pledge to Reform Canada's Elections," *Toronto Star*, February 1, 2017, https://www.thestar.com/news/canada/2017/02/01/trudeau-drops-pledge-to-reform-canadas-electoral-system-in-his-first-term.html.

84 So why did: Aaron Wherry, "How Trudeau Lost His Way on Electoral Reform," CBC, June 27, 2017, https://www.cbc.ca/news/politics/trudeau-electoral-reform-wherry-analysis-1.4179928.

85 As Andrew Coyne: Andrew Coyne, "Andrew Coyne: Trudeau's Petulant, Tone-Deaf Performance a Remarkable Milestone," *National Post*, June 28, 2017, https://nationalpost.com/

opinion/andrew-coyne-trudeaus-petulant-tone
-deaf-performance-a-remarkable-milestone.

86   "I make promises because": Boutilier and
Ballingall, "Trudeau Insists Election Reform
Still on Table."

87   "As far as Canada Post": Ryan Maloney,
"Liberal Plan on Door-to-Door Mail Delivery
Puts Spotlight on Campaign Pledges,"
Huffington Post Canada, January 24, 2018,
https://www.huffingtonpost.ca/2018/01/24/
liberal-plan-on-door-to-door-delivery-puts
-spotlight-on-campaign-pledges_a_23342683/.
The quote can also be heard during the CPAC
press conference in Montreal, QC, September
3, 2015, http://www.cpac.ca/en/programs/
leaders-tour/episodes/90005882.

87   "Those households that were": Maloney,
"Liberal Plan on Door-to-Door Mail Delivery
Puts Spotlight on Campaign Pledges."

88   "No veteran will be forced": Lee
Berthiaume, "Veterans Await Details of
Long-Promised Disability Pension Plan,"
The Star, December 19, 2017, https://www
.thestar.com/news/canada/2017/12/19/
veterans-await-details-of-long-promised
-disability-pension-plan.html.

88   "Why are we still fighting": Emily Mertz,
"Injured Veteran That Questioned Trudeau
During Edmonton Town Hall Says 'Enough
Is Enough,'" Global News, February 2,
2018, https://globalnews.ca/news/4003755/
injured-veteran-edmonton-town-hall-justin
-trudeau/.

89   "We will make": 2015 Liberal Party Platform,
accessed June 13, 2019, https://www.liberal.ca/
realchange/free-votes.

89   "MP Kicked Off Two Committees": Bobbi-Jean
MacKinnon, "New Brunswick MP Kicked
Off Two Committees for Breaking Liberal
Ranks on Tax Changes," CBC News, October
5, 2017, https://www.cbc.ca/news/canada/new
-brunswick/wayne-long-liberal-mp-committee
-business-tax-1.4342744.

91   "I am very much in favour": Krista Balsom,
"Politics, Passion & Pipelines: An Interview
with Justin," *Your McMurray Magazine*, May
28, 2014, https://yourmcmurraymagazine
.com/archives/features/323/politics-passion
-pipelines-an-interview-with-justin-trudeau.

91   "Energy East's pipeline": Annie Mathieu,
"*Justin Trudeau au Soleil: Énergie Est n'est pas
socialement acceptable*" [Justin Trudeau to Soleil:
Energy East Is Not Socially Acceptable],
Le Soleil, December 13, 2014, https://www
.lesoleil.com/actualite/politique/justin-trudeau
-au-soleil-energie-est-nest-pas-socialement
-acceptable-36ba5253f2e35e780cb6cf44f6
a2c545.

92   "You cannot play favourites": Justin Trudeau,
interview by George Stroumboulopoulos,
George Stroumboulopoulos Tonight, CBC, April
1, 2014, video, https://www.cbc.ca/strombo/
videos/justin-trudeau-michael-ignatieff.

92   "Canada isn't doing well": Know Nothing,
"Justin Trudeau—Alberta vs Quebec," *Tele-
Québec*, YouTube video, 0:38, July 14, 2014,
https://www.youtube.com/watch?v=5vAlz1at
_OU.

93   "Is Canada": Martin Patriquin, "Justin Trudeau
Apologizes After One Pander Too Many,"
Maclean's, November 23, 2012, https://www
.macleans.ca/politics/ottawa/justin-trudeau
-one-pander-too-many/.

93   "I am Liberal": Ibid.

94   Turns out that Justin's: Éric Grenier, "Why the
Senate Is Unpredictable—and Its Independents
Not So Independent," CBC News, June 19,
2017, https://www.cbc.ca/news/politics/grenier
-senators-votes-1.4162949.

SUNNY WAYS!

97   "We . . . made a commitment": Justin Trudeau,
"Prime Minister Justin Trudeau's Open letter
to Canadians," Liberal.ca, November 4, 2015,
https://www.liberal.ca/prime-minister-justin
-trudeaus-open-letter-to-canadians/.

98 "It is not my practice": Rachel Aiello, "Kenney Apologizes for Personal Attack on PM Trudeau," CTV News, May 24, 2018, https://www.ctvnews.ca/politics/kenney-apologizes-for-personal-attack-on-pm-trudeau-1.3944118.

99 "You are a piece": "Trudeau Calls Kent a 'Piece of Sh**' in House of Commons," CBC News, December 14, 2011, https://www.ctvnews.ca/trudeau-calls-kent-a-piece-of-sh-in-house-of-commons-1.740571.

100 "Sunny ways, my friends": Mark Gollom, "Justin Trudeau Pledges 'Real Change' as Liberals Leap Ahead to Majority Government," CBC News, October 19, 2015, https://www.cbc.ca/news/politics/canada-election-2015-voting-results-polls-1.3278537.

101 "The challenge that I have": Justin Trudeau, "Justin Trudeau Takes a Gamble on Staying Positive," interview by Peter Mansbridge, CBC News, April 17, 2013, video, 6:35, https://www.cbc.ca/news/canada/justin-trudeau-takes-a-gamble-on-staying-positive-1.1357601.

102 "We didn't join them": Meagan Campbell, "Justin Trudeau Tells Convention the Conservatives Are Still 'Harper's Party': Speech Transcript," *Maclean's*, April 21, 2018, https://www.macleans.ca/politics/ottawa/justin-trudeau-convention-speech-transcript/.

102 "If there's one": Ibid.

103 "I found Harper": Gloria Galloway, "Mulcair Looks Back on His Own Successes as New Democrats Choose His Successor," *Globe and Mail*, September 28, 2017, https://www.theglobeandmail.com/news/politics/mulcair-looks-back-on-his-own-successes-as-new-democrats-choose-his-successor/article36423809/.

104 "When you put a price": Richard Zussman, "Blame Game Continues as Gas Prices Keep Soaring in Metro Vancouver," Global News, April 30, 2018, https://globalnews.ca/news/4177647/metro-vancouver-gas-prices-fault/.

105 "Trudeau Family Getting": Catherine Tunney, "Trudeau Family Getting Its Meals Delivered from 24 Sussex to Rideau Cottage," CBC News, May 3, 2018, https://www.cbc.ca/news/politics/24-sussex-meals-rideau-cottage-1.4643358.

106 "Canada's Access-To-Information": Laura Stone, "Canada's Access-to-Information System Has Worsened Under Trudeau Government," *Globe and Mail*, September 27, 2017, https://www.theglobeandmail.com/news/politics/canadas-access-to-information-system-has-worsened-under-trudeau-government-report/article36407309/.

WOKE BAE

109 "Peoplekind": Rebecca Joseph, "Justin Trudeau's 'Peoplekind' Remark Draws Ridicule in U.S. and U.K. Media," Global News, February 6, 2018, https://globalnews.ca/news/4009843/justin-trudeau-peoplekind-piers-morgan/. The quote was also covered in the *Washington Post*, *New York Times*, *Toronto Star*, *The Guardian*, *The Telegraph*, *BBC News*, *Herald Sun*, *Chicago Tribune*, *etc.*, *etc.* Alt-right nazis, all of 'em!

110 Young woman asking: "Justin Trudeau: 'Peoplekind' Not 'Mankind'" BBC News, 0:36, February 7, 2018, available at: https://www.youtube.com/watch?v=ItsGW1Nlm3c.

111 "There's lots of things": Andree Lau, "Justin Trudeau Teaches Men How to Be Better Feminists in 10 Seconds," *Huffington Post Canada*, April 30, 2016, https://www.huffingtonpost.ca/2016/04/30/justin-trudeau-feminist-advice-snapchat_n_9815126.html.

112 "alt-right nazis": "Trudeau Advisor Labels All Critics of 'Peoplekind' Remark as Nazis. Shapiro Must Be Surprised," *Daily Wire*, February 8, 2018, https://www.dailywire.com/news/26914/trudeau-advisor-labels-all-critics-peoplekind-daily-wire.

112 In 2018, Service Canada: Canadian Press, "Service Canada Employees Asked to Avoid Using Mr., Mrs., or Ms. as well as Mother and Father," Global News, March 21, 2018, https://globalnews.ca/news/4097862/service-canada-gender-neutral-language/.

113 "Will the same standard": Justin Trudeau, "The House Sits Down with the Prime Minister," *The House*, CBC Radio, February 3, 2018, https://www.cbc.ca/radio/thehouse/the-house-sits-down-with-the-prime-minister-1.4512987/the-house-sits-down-with-the-prime-minister-1.4517766.

114 "I've been working": Ibid.

115 "It's not a rare incident": Douglas Quan, Adrian Humphreys, and Marie-Danielle Smith, "Why an 18-Year-Old Groping Allegation Against Justin Trudeau Is Not a #MeToo Moment," *National Post*, June 22, 2018, http://nationalpost.com/news/politics/why-an-18-year-old-groping-allegation-against-justin-trudeau-is-not-a-metoo-moment.

116 "I'm sorry. If I had": Ibid.

116 "people experience things": Chris Herhalt, "Don't Investigate Groping Allegation from 2000, Trudeau Says," CP24, July 6, 2018, https://www.cp24.com/news/don-t-investigate-groping-allegation-from-2000-trudeau-says-1.4002639.

117 The editor and the newspaper: Quan, Humphreys, and Smith, "Why an 18-Year-Old Groping Allegation Against Justin Trudeau Is Not a #MeToo Moment."

118 "If you had to predict": "Prime Minister Justin Trudeau," *Live with Kelly and Ryan*, June 5, 2017, YouTube video, 3:32, available at: https://www.youtube.com/watch?v=p5R1lMOhwpc.

120 "Canada has become": Wilfrid Laurier, speech, Cornwall, Ontario, September 30, 1908, quoted in Patrice Dutil and David Clark MacKenzie, *Canada 1911: The Decisive Election That Shaped the Country* (Toronto: Dundrun Press, 2011), 31.

120 "I look at what": Justine Trudeau, "Prime Minister Justin Trudeau," *60 Minutes*, CBS News, March 6, 2016, https://www.cbsnews.com/news/60-minutes-prime-minister-trudeau/.

OUR HOME ON NATIVE LAND

122 "Why doesn't the prime": Peter Zimonjic, "MP Drops F-bomb in Commons, Accuses Trudeau of Not Caring About Indigenous Rights," CBC News, September 25, 2018, https://www.cbc.ca/news/politics/romeo-saganash-f-bomb-house-commons-1.4838124.

123 "A place to store": Justin Trudeau, speech, Saskatoon Town Hall, January 25, 2017, quoted in John Paul Tasker, "Trudeau's 'Canoes and Paddles' Remark Called Borderline Racist By First Nations MP," CBC News, February 17, 2017, https://www.cbc.ca/news/politics/saganash-letter-trudeau-canoe-paddles-1.3976685.

125 "I've spoken with": Ibid.

126 "A sacred obligation": Susana Mas, "Trudeau Lays Out Plan for New Relationship with Indigenous People," CBC News, December 8, 2015, https://www.cbc.ca/news/politics/justin-trudeau-afn-indigenous-aboriginal-people-1.3354747.

127 "Canada Has Spent $110,000": Ashifa Kassam, "Canada Has Spent $110,000 to Avoid Paying $6,000 for Indigenous Teen's Orthodontics," *The Guardian*, September 30, 2017, https://www.theguardian.com/world/2017/sep/30/canada-first-nations-orthodontics-teenager.

128 "I said, we're": "Justin Trudeau On Boxing Match's Side Bets," Althiaraj, YouTube video, 1:40, March 31, 2012, https://www.youtube.com/watch?v=CEImRJxK-9Y#t=46.

129 "It wasn't random": Stephen Rodrick, "Justin Trudeau: The North Star," *Rolling Stone*, July 26, 2017, https://www.rollingstone.com/politics/politics-features/justin-trudeau-the-north-star-194313/.

130 "Thank you very": "Justin Trudeau Tells Protester 'thank you for your donation,'" *National Post*, YouTube video, 1:17, March 28, 2019, https://www.youtube.com/watch?v=qcvxEu0jpKo.

JUSTIN & THE MEDIA: A LOVE STORY

134 Is it impolite: "CBC's Peter Mansbridge Officiated Wedding for Trudeau's Communications Director," *Toronto Sun*, November 11, 2015, https://torontosun.com/2015/11/11/cbcs-peter-mansbridge-officiated-wedding-for-trudeaus-communications-director/wcm/4cb39d10-14f3-4d4a-8396-c4450cb12f14.

135 "What shampoo do you": Justin Trudeau, "'Plane Talk' with Justin Trudeau: When He Lies, His Biggest Regret and Greatest Extravagance," interview by Tom Clark, Global News, September 21, 2014, transcript, https://globalnews.ca/news/1574882/plane-talk-with-justin-trudeau-when-he-lies-his-biggest-regret-and-greatest-extravagance/.

136 "Our New Political Crush": *Elle*, "Justin Trudeau Is Our New Political Crush," YouTube video, 1:30, March 2, 2017, https://www.youtube.com/watch?v=oBtqgcgjr4Y.

137 "Couple of praise points": News Conference—Justin Trudeau in Shelburne, N.S, CPAC, video, 18:34, July 21, 2017, http://www.cpac.ca/en/programs/headline-politics/episodes/52131072.

138 "Justin Trudeau offered": StevenChase (Steven Chase), Twitter, December 7, 2017, 7:30 a.m., https://twitter.com/stevenchase/status/938747488378544129.

138 "forced on us": @StevenChase (Steven Chase), "Justin Trudeau offered . . ." Twitter, December 7, 2017, 11:41 a.m, https://twitter.com/stevenchase/status/938855906061758464.

139 "Because I am": "Scrums," CPAC, video, 28:30, February 25, 2014, http://www.cpac.ca/en/programs/scrums/episodes/30901661. Note: This was answered in French, another English translation is "Well, I'm a federal politician and I want to become prime minister, so I think it would be very inappropriate for me to take a firm position now."

142 "If Trudeau Is": Terry Glavin, "If Trudeau Is the Free World's Last Hope, the Free World Is Doomed," *National Post*, August 2, 2017, https://nationalpost.com/opinion/terry-glavin-if-trudeau-is-the-free-worlds-last-hope-the-free-world-is-doomed.

142 "He says one thing": Vinay Menon, "For the Sake of Peoplekind, Justin Trudeau Needs to Shut His Mouth," *Toronto Star*, February 7, 2018, https://www.thestar.com/entertainment/opinion/2018/02/07/for-the-sake-of-peoplekind-justin-trudeau-needs-to-shut-up.html.

142 "He doesn't have": Lysiane Gagnon, "He's Sweet, But Is Trudeau a PM?" *Globe and Mail*, October 22, 2014, https://www.theglobeandmail.com/opinion/hes-sweet-but-is-trudeau-a-pm/article21200020/.

OTHER PEOPLE'S MONEY

144 "Liberal Spending Review": Bill Curry, "Liberal Spending Review So Far Identifies No Cuts, But Highlights New Spending," *Globe and Mail*, March 12, 2018, https://www.theglobeandmail.com/politics/article-liberal-spending-review-so-far-identifies-no-cuts-but-highlights-new/.

144 "A Liberal government": Ibid.

145 "The budget will balance": *Primetime Politics with Peter Van Dusen*, CPAC, video, February 11, 2014, http://www.cpac.ca/en/programs/primetime-politics/episodes/30396042.

146 "I've committed to continuing": Paul Well, "The Making of a Prime Minister: Inside Trudeau's Epic Win," *Maclean's*, October

21, 2015, https://site.macleans.ca/longform/
trudeau/.

147 "I am looking straight": "Replay: The Globe
and Mail Election Leaders' Debate 2015,"
Globe and Mail, YouTube video, 2:18:15,
September 17, 2015, https://www.youtube.com/
watch?v=XbnMz7tsXjo.

148 Justin inherited a $7.5: Andy Blatchford,
"Despite $7.5B Surplus, Liberals Insist They're
Left with a Deficit," Global News, April 29,
2016, https://globalnews.ca/news/2671448/
despite-7-5b-surplus-liberals-insist-theyre-left
-with-a-deficit/.

148 During the 2015 campaign: "Justin Trudeau
Says Liberals Plan 3 Years of Deficits to
Push Infrastructure," CBC News, August
27, 2015, https://www.cbc.ca/news/politics/
canada-election-2015-liberals-infrastructure
-deficits-1.3205535.

148 Unfortunately, Justin's carefully: Canadian
Press, "Federal Budget 2017: Trudeau
Government Projects $28.5 Billion Deficit in
2017–2018," Global News, March 22, 2017,
https://globalnews.ca/news/3327930/federal
-budget-2017-liberals-raising-ei-premiums
-and-hiking-taxes-on-smokes-booze/.

148 The 2019 budget . . .: "Finance Minister
Defends Liberal Budget Measures as Sales
Effort Gets Underway," Canada's National
Observer, March 20, 2019, https://www
.nationalobserver.com/2019/03/20/news/
finance-minister-defends-liberal-budget
-measures-sales-effort-gets-underway.

148 The timeline for: Bill Curry, "Deficit on
Track for Elimination by 2045, a Decade
Earlier Than Last Year's Projection," Globe
and Mail, December 22, 2017, https://www
.theglobeandmail.com/news/politics/deficit-on
-track-for-elimination-by-2045-a-decade-earlier
-than-last-years-projection/article37420980/.

149 In April 2019, The International: Associated
Press, "IMF Cuts Forecast for 2019 Growth
in Canada, World," CBS, January 21, 2019,
https://www.cbc.ca/news/business/imf-global
-growth-1.4986550.

149 Canada's GDP: "Canada: Economic and
Financial Data," accessed March 19, 2019,
https://www150.statcan.gc.ca/n1/en/dsbbcan.

149 Federal deficit: "Equality + Growth: A Strong
Middle Class," Department of Finance Canada,
Minister of Finance, William Francis Morneau,
February 27, 2018, https://www.budget.gc.ca/
2018/docs/plan/budget-2018-en.pdf.

149 Provincial deficit: Fiscal Reference
Tables,-2018: Part 5-9, Department of Finance,
accessed April 19, 2019, https://www.fin.gc.ca/
frt-trf/2018/frt-trf-1805-eng.asp#tbl31.

149 would grow 1.5 per cent: Jordan Press, "Federal
Budget Won't Be Balanced until 2040, Finance
Department Says," Global News, December
21, 2018, https://globalnews.ca/news/4787265/
federal-budget-balance-2040/.

150 "We can grow": Canadian Press, "Trudeau
Says Liberals Determined to Grow Economy
'From the Heart Outwards,'" CTV News,
August 12, 2015, https://www.ctvnews
.ca/politics/election/trudeau-says-liberals
-determined-to-grow-economy-from-the
-heart-outwards-1.2513674.

152 Mike Duffy: Althia Raj, "Mike Duffy
Investigation, Trial Cost RCMP $477,858,"
Huffington Post Canada, June 23, 2016, https://
www.huffingtonpost.ca/2016/06/23/mike-duffy
-investigation-rcmp-costs_n_10638876.html.

153 "BFF in the PMO": Adam Radwanski,
"Gerald Butts: The BFF in the PMO," Globe
and Mail, September 2, 2016, https://www
.theglobeandmail.com/news/gerald-butts
-the-guardian-of-the-trudeunarrative/
article31692482/.

153 "puppet-master": Lee Berthiaume,
"Archival: Why Gerald Butts Was Trudeau's
Most Trusted Adviser," Ottawa Citizen,
October 21, 2014, https://ottawacitizen

.com/news/politics/the-man-behind-the
-curtain-why-gerald-butts-is-trudeaus
-most-trusted-adviser.

153 "perhaps the most powerful": Nick Taylor-
Vaisey, "Gerald Butts's Sprawling, Heavy-
Hitting, Mega-Rich, Do-Gooder Rolodex,"
Maclean's, October 12, 2017, https://www
.macleans.ca/politics/ottawa/the-impressive
-network-of-gerald-butts/.

153 When Butts moved: Joanne Seiff, "Moving
for Work Comes at a Cost—But $126K Is a
Little Rich, Joanne Seiff Says," CBC News,
October 1, 2016, https://www.cbc.ca/news/
canada/manitoba/canada-moving-costs-trudeau
-government-1.3786877.

153 Instead, Butts simply: Joan Bryden, "Top
Two PMO Aides Apologize for Controversy
Over Moving Expenses," *Canada's National
Observer*, September 23, 2016, https://www
.nationalobserver.com/2016/09/22/news/top
-two-pmo-aides-apologize-controversy-over
-moving-expenses.

154 "Fairness for middle class": Justin
Trudeau, "Justin Trudeau on Fairness
for the Middle Class," Liberal.ca, https://
www.liberal.ca/realchange/justin-trudeau
-on-fairness-for-the-middle-class/
(accessed March 3, 2019).

156 The Liberal Party: Andrew Coyne, "Andrew
Coyne: Bloated, Glossy $212,000 Federal
Budget Cover a Fitting Symbol of Modern
Government" National Post, October 25,
2017, https://nationalpost.com/opinion/
andrew-coyne-bloated-glossy-212000
-federal-budget-cover-a-fitting-symbol-of
-modern-government.

159 "Well, deficits are": "Interview with Justin
Trudeau," *West Block*, Global News, September
26, 2015, available at: https://www.youtube
.com/watch?v=py1t3tGqCuk.

160 "Sorry I can't be": @Justin Trudeau (Justin
Trudeau), Twitter, December 2, 2018, 5:00

a.m., https://twitter.com/justintrudeau/
status/1069214653169844227?.

161 As Justin's office: Janice Dickson, "Trudeau
Criticized for Tweet to Trevor Noah Pledging
Money for Cause," Toronto Star, December
3, 2018, https://www.thestar.com/news/
canada/2018/12/03/trudeau-criticized-for
-tweet-to-trevor-noah-pledging-money-for
-cause.html.

161 Justin's $50 million: Janice Dickson, "Trudeau
Criticized for Tweet to Trevor Noah Pledging
$50M Charity Gift," CBC, December 3, 2018,
https://www.cbc.ca/news/politics/trudeau
-trevor-noah-money-1.4930216.

162 "One of the things": Kevin Carmichael,
"Justin Trudeau Claims to Be a Fiscal
Conservative. He's Not," *Maclean's*, April 26,
2016, https://www.macleans.ca/economy/
business/justin-trudeau-claims-to-be-a-fiscal
-conservative-hes-not/.

JUSTIN & HIS SOCKS: A TALE FOR THE AGES

166 "Canada's Justin Trudeau": Mikey Smith,
"Canada's Justin Trudeau Is Wearing
Chewbacca Socks and Everybody's
Freaking Out," *Daily Mirror*, September
20, 2017, https://www.mirror.co.uk/news/
politics/canadas-justin-trudeau-wearing
-chewbacca-11208246.

166 "Justin Trudeau's Zany": Raisa Bruner, "Justin
Trudeau's Zany's 'Star Wars' Sock Choice
Is Throwing the Internet for a Loop," *Time*,
September 20, 2017, http://time.com/4950653/
justin-trudeau-chewbacca-socks/.

166 "Justin Trudeau's 'Star Wars'": Ryan
Parker, "Justin Trudeau's 'Star Wars'
Chewbacca Socks Create Social Media
Stir," *Hollywood Reporter*, September 20,
2017, https://www.hollywoodreporter
.com/heat-vision/star-wars-justin-trudeaus
-chewbacca-socks-cause-social-media
-nerdgasm-1041504.

166 "No World Leader's Socks": Dominique Mosbergen, "Justin Trudeau's Socks Are on Point," *Huffington Post Canada*, June 23, 2017, https://www.huffingtonpost.ca/entry/justin-trudeau-socks_n_594cb905e4b0da2c731aae88.

167 "Justin Trudeau's Socks Appeal": Vinay Menon, "Justin Trudeau's Socks Appeal Is Starting to Wear Thin," *Toronto Star*, June 28, 2017, https://www.thestar.com-entertainment/2017/06/28/justin-trudeaus-socks-appeal-is-starting-to-wear-thin-menon.html.

170 "I am a Canadian": John Diefenbaker, House of Commons (July 1, 1960).

170 "I've also had": Karl Moore, "One-on-One Interview with Justin Trudeau," *Forbes*, November 4, 2015, https://www.forbes.com/sites/karlmoore/2015/11/04/an-one-on-one-with-canadas-new-prime-minister-justin-trudeau/#b534995ea062.

"ETHICS"

174 "Conservative ethics abuses": @JustinTrudeau (Justin Trudeau), Twitter, October 22, 2013, 3:45 p.m., https://twitter.com/justintrudeau/status/392783681892265984?.

174 Not just once: Katie Dangerfield, "Trudeau's Cabinet Faces 5th Ethics Investigation—Here's How Stephen Harper's Office Compared," Global News, February 13, 2019, https://globalnews.ca/news/4951921/justin-trudeau-ethics-investigation-stephen-harper/.

175 "I am committed to leading": Justin Trudeau, "Prime Minister Justin Trudeau's Open Letter to Canadians," Liberal.ca, November 4, 2015, https://www.liberal.ca/prime-minister-justin-trudeaus-open-letter-to-canadians/.

176 "Prime Minister, you talk": "FactPointVideo," "Trudeau Dodges Questions Over Tax Benefits He Receives Through Family Trusts." YouTube video, 1:38, September 19, 2017, https://www.youtube.com/watch?v=8yH-Ep4Kj-c.

177 "I no longer have dealings": Ibid.

178 "A large percentage": Justin Trudeau, interview by Peter Mansbridge, *The National*, CBC, 7:25, September 8, 2015, available at: https://www.youtube.com/watch?v=lkMa8UcABnA.

180 "Low-income families": "Low-income Families 'Don't Benefit' from Tax Breaks: Trudeau" Global News, video 1:22, February 5, 2019, https://globalnews.ca/video/4927706/low-income-families-dont-benefit-from-tax-breaks-trudeau.

182 The Conflict of Interest: David Akins, "Ethics Watchdog Wants to Talk to Bill Morneau About His 2015 Stock Trades," Global News, December 1, 2017, https://globalnews.ca/news/3893089/ethics-watchdog-morneau-stock-trades/.

WISH YOU WERE HERE!
JUSTIN'S ISLAND GETAWAY

185 "We don't see an issue": Dehaas, Josh. "PM Admits He Took Billionaire's Helicopter to Private Island" CTVNews, January 12, 2017, https://www.ctvnews.ca/politics/pm-admits-he-took-billionaire-s-helicopter-to-private-island-1.3238837.

186 "accept travel on non-commercial": Conflicts of Interest Rules, S.C. 2006, c. 9, s. 2, §12, available at: https://laws-lois.justice.gc.ca/eng/acts/C-36.65/page-2. html?txthl=influence+seek&wbdisable=true.

187 "supposed ethical issues": *Global National*, Global News, 6:41, December 20, 2017, https://globalnews.ca/video/4783819/global-national-dec-20-6.

188 The added cost of Justin's: Elizabeth Thompson, "CBC Investigates: Trudeau's Bahamas Vacation Cost Over $215K—Far More Than Initially Disclosed," CBC, September 13, 2017, https://www.cbc.ca/news/politics/trudeau-bahamas-vacation-rcmp-1.4286033.

188 Justin's use of . . . : Josh Dehaas, "PM's Use of Jet for Family Vacation Emitted as much CO2 as Average Canadian Per Year," CTV News, January 20, 2017, https://www.ctvnews.ca/mobile/politics/pm-s-use-of-jet-for-family-vacation-emitted-as-much-co2-as-average-canadian-per-year-1.3250397.

189 "I also want to know": Hélène Buzzetti, "*Les Conservateurs Veulent Forcer Trudeau à Témoigner*" [Conservatives Want to Force Trudeau to Testify], *Le Devoir*, January 6, 2018, https://www.ledevoir.com/politique/canada/516910/conflit-d-interets-les-conservateurs-veulent-forcer-trudeau-a-comparaitre.

190 "On December 20, 2017": Conflicts of Interest Rules, S.C. 2006, c. 9, s. 2, §§5, 11, 12, 21.

190 "Mr. Trudeau failed to meet": Office of the Conflict of Interest and Ethics Commissioner, Mary Dawson, *The Trudeau Report* (Ottawa, Ontario: Parliament of Canada, 2017), http://ciec-ccie.parl.gc.ca/Documents/English/Public%20Reports/Examination%20Reports/The%20Trudeau%20Report.pdf.

190 "I found that these gifts": Ibid.

191 "Mr. Trudeau contravened": Ibid.

191 "I found that Mr. Trudeau": Ibid.

191 "Mr. Trudeau failed to arrange": Ibid.

193 "How could that not": "Justin Trudeau Fumbles Question About His Conflict of Interest," YouTube video, 0:19, December 20, 2017, https://www.youtube.com/watch?v=15-5O4UPM0U.

194 "Aga Khan is": Ibid.

195 "What's your greatest": Justin Trudeau, "'Plane Talk' with Justin Trudeau: When He Lies, His Biggest Regret and Greatest Extravagance," interview by Tom Clark, September 21, 2014, Global News, https://globalnews.ca/news/1574882/plane-talk-with-justin-trudeau-when-he-lies-his-biggest-regret-and-greatest-extravagance/.

196 "I think people are": Guy Lawson, "Trudeau's Canada, Again," *New York Times Magazine*, December 8, 2015, https://www.nytimes.com/2015/12/13/magazine/trudeaus-canada-again.html.

YOUR PRIME MINISTER IN ACTION!

198 The number of: Canadian Press, "Trudeau Dodges Pledge to Meet with Ethics Commissioner over Aga Khan Vacation," CP24, January 9, 2018, https://www.cp24.com/news/trudeau-dodges-pledge-to-meet-with-ethics-commissioner-over-aga-khan-vacation-1.3751791.

198 No one knows: Laura Stone, "Ethics Commissioner Mary Dawson Says She 'Went Out with a Bang'" *Globe and Mail*, January 5, 2018, https://www.theglobeandmail.com/news/politics/ethics-commissioner-mary-dawson-says-she-went-out-with-a-bang/article37517088/.

199 "How many times did": Geoff Regan, 42 House of Commons Debate 1, *Hansard* 148, no. 174 (May 10, 2017), http://www.ourcommons.ca/DocumentViewer/en/42-1/house/sitting-174/hansard.

201 Question Period, House of Commons: Ibid.

STOP THE PRESSES!

208 She became concerned: Alastair Sharp and Mike De Souza, "New Audio of Phone Call Reveals Jody Wilson-Raybould's Warning about SNC-Lavalin Prosecution," National Observer, March 29, 2019, https://www.nationalobserver.com/2019/03/29/news/new-audio-phone-call-reveals-jody-wilson-rayboulds-warning-about-snc-lavalin.

208 SNC-Lavalin, which: " A Closer Look at SNC-Lavalin's Sometimes Murky Past," CBC News, February 8, 2019, https://www.cbc.ca/news/canada/snc-lavalin-corruption-fraud-bribery-libya-muhc-1.5010865.

208 SNC-Lavalin had: Tom Parkin, "What Did the Liberals see in SNC-Lavalin? A Company

in Need of a Bailout," *Maclean's*, February 14, 2019, https://www.macleans.ca/opinion/what-did-the-liberals-see-in-snc-lavalin-a-company-in-need-of-a-bailout/.

208 After Wilson-Raybould refused: Rahul Kalvapalle and Amanda Connolly, "Jody Wilson-Raybould and Jane Philpott kicked out of Liberal Party Caucus," Global News, April 2, 2019, https:// globalnews.ca/news/5123526/liberal-caucus-wilson-raybould-jane-philpott/.

208 And yet, a Liberal: Mike Blanchfield, "Liberal-Stacked Justice Committee Shuts Down SNC-Lavalin Investigation," *Huffington Post Canada*, February 27, 2019, https://www.huffingtonpost.ca/2019/03/19/liberals-justice-committee-snc-lavalin_a_23695755/.

Photo Credits

Text

Page 78 (Top Right)   Justin Trudeau costume: Courtesy of Justin Tang/Canadian Press
Page 78 (Bottom)   Justin Trudeau in Indigenous headdress: Courtesy of Jeff McIntosh/Canadian Press
Page 119   Kim Campbell: Courtesy of University Communications/ Simon Fraser University
Page 120 (Left)   Sir Wilfred Laurier: Courtesy of British Library/Public Domain
Page 120 (Right)   Justin Trudeau: Courtesy of Chris Wattie/Reuters
Page 129   Trudeau boxing and tattoo: Courtesy of Sean Kilpatrick/Canadian Press
Page 140 (Left)   Wayne Gretzky wiping tears: Courtesy of Adrian Wyld/Canadian Press
Page 140 (Right)   Justin Trudeau crying: Courtesy of Adrian Wyld/Canadian Press
Page 155 (Top)   Mike Duffy: Courtesy of Blair Gable/Reuters
Page 155 (Bottom)   Gerald Butts: Courtesy of Sean Kilpatrick/Canadian Press
Page 157   Cover of budget: Courtesy of Adrian Wyld/Canadian Press
Page 165   Trudeau joking with Boissonnault as they compare socks during pride ceremony: Courtesy of Adrian Wyld/Canadian Press
Page 169 (Top Left)   Chewbacca socks: Courtesy of John Moore/Getty Images
Page 169 (Top Right)   Jolly Rogers socks: Courtesy of Andrew Vaughan/Canadian Press
Page 169 (Middle Left)   Moose socks: Courtesy Leon Neal/Getty Images
Page 169 (Middle Right)   Rubber ducky socks: Courtesy of Fabrice Coffrini/Getty Images
Page 169 (Bottom Left)   R2-D2 and C-3PO socks: Courtesy of Paul Chiasson/Canadian Press
Page 169 (Bottom Right)   Ramadan socks: Courtesy of Nathan Denette/Canadian Press
Page 171 (Top)   John G. Diefenbaker: Courtesy of Gar Lunney/Library and Archives Canada/ Public Domain
Page 171 (Bottom)   Justin Trudeau: Courtesy of Chris Wattie/Reuters

Mini Heads

Yelling Justin Trudeau: Courtesy of Chris Wattie/Reuters
Funny face Justin Trudeau: Courtesy of Chris Wattie/Reuters
Screaming Justin Trudeau: Courtesy of Chris Wattie/Reuters
Angry Justin Trudeau: South China Morning/Getty Images
Trudeau smiling with beer: Courtesy of Paul Chiasson/Canadian Press
Trudeau smiling while praying: Courtesy of Christinne Muschi/Reuters
Justin Trudeau duck face: Courtesy of Fred Chartrand/Canadian Press

About the Author

Ian Ferguson won the Stephen Leacock Medal for Humour for his book *Village of the Small Houses*, and is the coauthor, with his brother Will Ferguson, of *How to Be a Canadian*, which was shortlisted for the Leacock and which won the CBA Libris Award for nonfiction. The follow-up, *Being Canadian: Your Guide to the Best* Country in the World*, is hot off the presses, as is the equally unhelpful *The Survival Guide to British Columbia*. Ian was a contributing essayist to *Me Funny*, a celebration of Aboriginal humour, was selected for inclusion in *The Penguin Anthology of Canadian Humour*, and was profiled in *Second Chapter: The Canadian Writers Photography Project*. His writing has appeared in *Reader's Digest*, *Maclean's*, the *Globe and Mail*, the *National Post*, and *enRoute Magazine*, among others. For the past ten years Ian has worked as a writer and creative director for film and television. He currently resides in a magical city on an exotic island in the Pacific Ocean . . . so, Victoria.